Safeguarding Against Scams and Frauds in the Digital Age

C. P. Kumar
Reiki Healer
Roorkee - 247667, India

Disclaimer

While every effort has been made to ensure the accuracy and completeness of the content in this book, the author cannot guarantee that the information contained herein is error-free, up-to-date, or suitable for every individual circumstance.

The author shall not be held liable or responsible for any errors or omissions in the content of the book, nor for any damages, or losses that may arise from any actions taken based upon the suggestions or contents presented in the book.

Readers are advised to use their own judgment and discretion in applying the information provided in this book, and to consult with qualified professionals before taking any action based on the contents of this book. The author disclaims any and all liability or responsibility for any actions taken or not taken based on the information contained in this book.

DEDICATION

To all those who have fallen victim to scams and frauds in the digital age,

This book is dedicated to you - the individuals whose trust was exploited, whose privacy was invaded, and whose hard-earned money was unjustly taken away. We stand in solidarity with your struggles and pledge to make a difference.

In a world that is rapidly evolving with technology, where every aspect of our lives is interconnected through the digital realm, the threats of scams and frauds have become more pervasive than ever before. It is essential to arm ourselves with knowledge and awareness to safeguard against these digital predators.

To those who have experienced the distressing consequences of identity theft, phishing scams, smishing, vishing, and fake social media profiles, we empathize with the emotional toll it has taken on you and your loved ones. To those who have been targeted by romance scams and deceived by AI-generated fake content, our hearts go out to you for the heartache caused.

To the victims of AI-driven fraud, whether it be chatbot scams, AI-powered phishing, or business email compromise, we understand the complexities of the ever-evolving digital landscape that you have faced.

To those who have lost their hard-earned money to investment scams, pyramid schemes, and fraudulent lotteries, we recognize the financial hardship you have endured. For those who have encountered the cunning tactics of charity scams and impersonation fraud, we admire your resilience in the face of such deceit.

To all the individuals affected by AI-enhanced credential stuffing, AI chatbot money doublers, and porn video call scams, we recognize the violation of your privacy and dignity.

Through the compilation of this book, our goal is to arm you with comprehensive knowledge and practical tools to protect yourselves and your loved ones from these digital threats. We dedicate our efforts to empowering you with the necessary insights to recognize and thwart scams and frauds in the digital age.

May this book serve as a beacon of hope and a shield of protection for you, as you navigate the intricate web of the digital world. Let us work together to create a safer digital ecosystem for generations to come.

With heartfelt dedication,

C. P. Kumar

CONTENTS

PREFACE

In an era dominated by technological advancements and digital interconnectedness, the world has witnessed a surge in scams and frauds that exploit unsuspecting individuals, leaving them vulnerable to financial losses, emotional distress, and compromised personal information. The pervasive nature of these deceptive practices calls for individuals to equip themselves with knowledge and tools to protect against such threats effectively.

This book, "Safeguarding Against Scams and Frauds in the Digital Age," serves as a comprehensive guide, navigating the intricate web of deceit woven by fraudsters in the digital realm. Its aim is to provide readers with a deep understanding of various scam tactics, ranging from traditional methods to the sophisticated approaches driven by artificial intelligence.

The book explores the devastating impact of identity theft, the deceptive techniques of phishing scams, and the dangers of AI-generated fake content like deepfakes. It delves into the emotional exploitation in romance scams, the role of AI-driven chatbots and robocalls, and the rise of tech support scams in a world of fake apps. Additionally, it uncovers the allure of false winnings in lottery and prize scams, the dangers of investment scams and pyramid schemes, and the misuse of philanthropy in charity scams.

As technology evolves, so do the scams, including AI-enhanced credential stuffing, impersonation tactics, AI chatbot money doublers, and explicit content scams. The book explores the potential risks associated with these AI-driven scams and the future trends in scams and fraud prevention.

Throughout its pages, the book empowers readers with practical tips, best practices, and insights to recognize, prevent, and combat scams effectively. By understanding the deceptive tactics employed by fraudsters and maintaining vigilance, readers can safeguard their digital lives and contribute to a safer online environment for all.

We hope this book will serve as a valuable resource to protect readers from falling victim to scams and frauds, enabling them to navigate the digital world with confidence and security. Let us collectively strive to stay ahead of the ever-evolving landscape of scams and frauds, ensuring a safer and more trustworthy digital age for everyone.

C. P. Kumar
Reiki Healer
Former Scientist 'G', National Institute of Hydrology
Roorkee - 247667, India
E-mail: cpkumar@yahoo.com
Web: https://www.angelfire.com/nh/cpkumar/virgo.html

Introduction

In our rapidly advancing digital era, technology has revolutionized the way we live, work, and communicate. The internet and various digital platforms have opened up incredible opportunities for convenience, connectivity, and productivity. However, along with these advancements, there is a darker side that poses significant threats to individuals and businesses alike – scams and fraud in the digital age. In this article, we will delve into the world of online scams and fraud, exploring their definitions, the evolving tactics scammers use, and the devastating impacts they can have on victims. Moreover, we will highlight the importance of safeguarding oneself against these threats to ensure a safer and more secure digital existence.

Understanding Scams and Fraud in the Digital Age

1. Definition of Scams and Fraud

Online scams and fraud refer to deceitful and malicious activities carried out through digital channels, intending to deceive individuals, gain unauthorized access to sensitive information, or exploit financial assets. These digital crimes can manifest in various forms, often leveraging the vast reach and anonymity of the internet.

2. The Pervasive Nature of Digital Scams and Fraud

As technology becomes increasingly integrated into our daily lives, so too does the prevalence of online scams and fraud. Cybercriminals adapt and evolve their tactics to exploit the vulnerabilities in technology and human behavior, making it crucial for individuals and organizations to remain vigilant.

The Evolution of Scams in the Digital Age

1. Phishing and Social Engineering

One of the most prevalent and enduring forms of digital scams is phishing. Cybercriminals use social engineering techniques to deceive individuals into divulging sensitive information, such as login credentials, personal data, or financial details. Phishing attempts often take the form of fraudulent emails, websites, or messages that appear legitimate.

2. Fake Websites and E-Commerce Scams

The rise of e-commerce has brought about an increase in fake websites designed to imitate legitimate online stores. Unsuspecting users may fall victim to purchasing counterfeit or non-existent products, leading to financial losses and compromised personal information.

3. Online Investment Scams

The allure of quick profits has led to the proliferation of online investment scams. Fraudsters create enticing investment opportunities that promise substantial returns, but in reality, these schemes are fraudulent and result in investors losing their money.

4. Romance Scams

Taking advantage of emotional vulnerability, romance scams involve cybercriminals developing false relationships with individuals, often leading to requests for money or personal information.

The Impact of Digital Scams and Fraud

1. Financial Losses

The immediate and most apparent impact of falling victim to digital scams is financial loss. Victims may lose substantial amounts of money through fraudulent transactions or unauthorized access to their bank accounts.

2. Identity Theft and Privacy Breaches

Scammers often aim to steal personal information, leading to identity theft. This can have long-term consequences, as stolen data may be used to commit various crimes, ranging from financial fraud to cyberbullying.

3. Emotional and Psychological Toll

Beyond financial losses, becoming a victim of a digital scam can have severe emotional and psychological repercussions. Feelings of shame, guilt, anger, and betrayal are common among victims, leading to a diminished sense of trust and security.

4. Damage to Reputation and Relationships

For businesses that fall prey to scams, there can be significant damage to their reputation and customer trust.

Such incidents can lead to a loss of clients, business opportunities, and overall credibility.

Safeguarding Against Digital Scams and Fraud

1. Education and Awareness

The first line of defense against digital scams is education and awareness. Individuals and organizations must be informed about the various types of scams and frauds prevalent in the digital age, as well as the tactics used by cybercriminals to deceive victims.

2. Strengthening Digital Literacy

Enhancing digital literacy is crucial to identify potential scams and suspicious activities online. Understanding how to verify the authenticity of websites, emails, and messages can help users avoid falling victim to phishing attempts.

3. Two-Factor Authentication (2FA)

Implementing two-factor authentication adds an extra layer of security to online accounts, making it harder for hackers to gain unauthorized access, even if they have obtained login credentials.

4. Secure Payment Methods

When making online transactions, users should opt for secure payment methods, such as credit cards or reputable online payment services, which offer additional protection against fraudulent charges.

5. Anti-Malware and Security Software

Installing reputable anti-malware and security software on devices can help detect and prevent phishing attempts, malware, and other cyber threats.

6. Vigilance and Reporting

Staying vigilant and reporting suspicious activities to appropriate authorities can aid in the identification and prevention of scams, protecting potential victims.

Conclusion

In the digital age, scams and fraud have become persistent threats that can affect anyone at any time. Cybercriminals are continually evolving their tactics, exploiting the convenience and anonymity provided by technology to target unsuspecting individuals and businesses. Understanding the various forms of digital scams, their impact, and how to safeguard against them is essential for maintaining a secure online presence. Through education, awareness, and proactive security measures, individuals and organizations can fortify their defenses and navigate the digital landscape with confidence and safety.

Introduction

In the fast-paced digital era, the rise of technological advancements has brought countless benefits and conveniences. However, it has also paved the way for various malicious activities, with identity theft being one of the most pervasive and detrimental cybercrimes. Identity theft is a growing concern that can wreak havoc on individuals and organizations alike, causing financial loss, emotional distress, and reputational damage. This article delves into the world of identity theft, exploring its definition, methods employed by perpetrators, the impact on victims, and effective strategies to safeguard against this ever-evolving threat.

Understanding Identity Theft

1. Definition and Scope

Identity theft refers to the unauthorized acquisition and use of an individual's personal information, such as their name, Social Security number, credit card details, or login credentials. The stolen data is then exploited for fraudulent purposes, including financial gain, illegal transactions, and impersonation.

2. Prevalence and Impact

Identity theft has become increasingly prevalent in the digital age due to the massive amount of personal data available online. From individuals to corporations, no one is immune to this threat. The consequences of identity theft can be far-reaching, resulting in financial ruin, legal entanglements, and emotional distress for victims.

Methods Employed by Perpetrators

1. Phishing Attacks

Phishing remains one of the most common tactics used by identity thieves. Perpetrators employ sophisticated techniques to deceive victims into divulging sensitive information through emails, fake websites, or social engineering. Unsuspecting users are tricked into providing their login credentials, credit card details, or other personal information, which is then exploited for illicit purposes.

2. Data Breaches

With the growing number of data breaches, cybercriminals gain access to vast databases of personal information. They capitalize on these data leaks to steal identities and carry out fraudulent activities. From financial institutions to social media platforms, any entity storing sensitive data can become a target.

3. Malware and Keyloggers

Malicious software, including keyloggers, Trojans, and spyware, allows cybercriminals to monitor and record victims' online activities without their knowledge. This enables identity thieves to intercept login credentials and financial information, which they can then misuse for their benefit.

4. Social Engineering

Identity thieves exploit human psychology through social engineering tactics. By impersonating trusted entities or manipulating victims' emotions, they coerce individuals into revealing their personal information willingly.

The Impact on Victims

1. Financial Loss

Identity theft can lead to significant financial losses, as perpetrators may use stolen information to conduct unauthorized transactions, open new credit accounts, or drain victims' bank accounts. These financial repercussions can take years to resolve fully.

2. Emotional Distress

Victims of identity theft often experience emotional distress, including feelings of violation, anxiety, and helplessness. The process of recovering their stolen identity and rectifying the damage can be emotionally taxing and time-consuming.

3. Legal Consequences

Identity theft can lead to legal repercussions for victims, especially if criminals commit crimes using stolen identities. Victims might find themselves entangled in legal battles to clear their name and restore their reputation.

4. Damaged Reputation

A tarnished reputation can have lasting effects on individuals and businesses. Identity theft can lead to false information being associated with a victim's name, causing reputational damage that is difficult to undo.

Safeguarding Against Identity Theft

1. Strong Passwords and Two-Factor Authentication

Using strong, unique passwords for every online account is essential. Additionally, enabling two-factor authentication provides an extra layer of security, making it significantly harder for attackers to gain unauthorized access.

2. Secure Internet Connections

Avoid accessing sensitive information or conducting financial transactions over public Wi-Fi networks. Instead, use a secure, password-protected connection or a Virtual Private Network (VPN) to protect your data from interception.

3. Regularly Monitor Financial Accounts

Frequently monitor bank statements, credit card transactions, and credit reports for any suspicious activity. Early detection can help mitigate the damage caused by identity theft.

4. Exercise Caution with Personal Information

Be cautious when sharing personal information online or over the phone. Only provide sensitive data to trusted and verified entities. Verify the legitimacy of websites and emails before sharing any information.

5. Update Software and Use Antivirus Protection

Keep your devices and software up to date to prevent vulnerabilities that could be exploited by hackers. Utilize reputable antivirus software to detect and remove malware effectively.

6. Shred Sensitive Documents

Dispose of paper documents containing personal information by shredding them before discarding them in the trash.

7. Be Wary of Social Engineering Tactics

Educate yourself and your employees about social engineering tactics and how to recognize and avoid them. Being cautious and verifying the identity of individuals and requests can thwart many identity theft attempts.

Conclusion

Identity theft remains a persistent threat in the digital age, endangering individuals and organizations worldwide. As technology continues to advance, so do the methods employed by cybercriminals. Safeguarding against identity theft requires vigilance, education, and the implementation of robust security measures. By staying informed about the latest trends in cybercrime and adopting preventive strategies, individuals and businesses can better protect themselves from the devastating consequences of identity theft in the digital era.

Introduction

In the rapidly evolving digital landscape, phishing scams pose a significant threat to online security. Phishing is a type of cybercrime where malicious actors use deceptive tactics to manipulate individuals into revealing sensitive information, such as passwords, credit card details, and personal data. This article aims to shed light on the tactics employed by phishers, the impact of phishing scams, and, most importantly, equip readers with practical strategies to safeguard against such threats.

Understanding Phishing Scams

Phishing scams rely on social engineering rather than technical vulnerabilities. They often involve the use of deceptive emails, instant messages, or fake websites that mimic trustworthy sources to lure victims into divulging sensitive information. Spear phishing, vishing, smishing, and pharming are some variations of phishing scams, each targeting different platforms and communication channels.

Spear Phishing: A targeted form of cyber attack that involves sending deceptive emails to specific individuals or organizations to trick them into revealing sensitive information or executing malicious actions.

Vishing: A type of cyber attack where attackers use voice communication, often through phone calls, to manipulate and deceive individuals into divulging personal or confidential information.

Smishing: A cyber attack method that involves sending fraudulent SMS messages to trick recipients into disclosing personal information, clicking on malicious links, or downloading harmful content.

Pharming: A cyber attack that redirects users to fraudulent websites or servers, often through DNS (Domain Name System) manipulation, with the aim of stealing sensitive data or spreading malware.

The Impact of Phishing Scams

Phishing scams can lead to significant financial losses for both individuals and businesses. Cybercriminals exploit stolen information to drain bank accounts, make unauthorized purchases, or commit identity theft. Moreover, falling victim to phishing attacks can result in reputational damage for businesses due to compromised customer data and loss of trust.

Recognizing Phishing Scams

Identifying phishing scams is crucial for safeguarding against them. There are several red flags to look out for in phishing emails, such as suspicious sender addresses, grammar errors, urgent calls to action, and requests for sensitive information. Additionally, recognizing fake websites can be done by checking for unsecured connections, misspelled URLs, and inconsistent branding.

Caller ID spoofing is a common tactic used in vishing scams, where attackers impersonate legitimate entities to trick individuals into disclosing sensitive information over the phone. Recognizing these tactics can help individuals protect themselves against vishing attempts.

Safeguarding Against Phishing Scams

Promoting security awareness is paramount in preventing phishing attacks. Providing cybersecurity training and conducting simulated phishing exercises can enhance individuals' and employees' awareness of phishing tactics.

Implementing multi-factor authentication (MFA) adds an extra layer of protection to online accounts, reducing the risk of unauthorized access even if login credentials are compromised.

Encouraging secure browsing practices, such as using HTTPS connections and avoiding clicking on links in unsolicited emails or messages, can help users stay safe online.

Employing email filtering and robust antivirus software can help detect and prevent phishing attacks from reaching users' inboxes or infecting their devices.

Reporting Phishing Scams

Reporting phishing scams is crucial for combating this menace. Individuals should report phishing attempts to relevant authorities, such as the Anti-Phishing Working Group (APWG) or the Internet Crime Complaint Center (IC3).

For phishing emails impersonating companies, notifying the organizations can help them take appropriate measures to protect their customers.

Conclusion

Phishing scams continue to pose a significant threat in the digital age, necessitating constant vigilance and proactive cybersecurity measures. By understanding phishing tactics, recognizing red flags, and adopting safeguarding strategies, individuals and businesses can fortify their defenses against this malicious menace. Through education, technology, and collective efforts to report phishing attempts, we can create a safer online environment for everyone, safeguarding against scams and frauds, and ensuring a more secure and trusted digital future.

Chapter 4. Smishing (SMS Phishing) and Vishing (Voice Phishing)

Introduction

In the ever-evolving landscape of digital communication and technology, cybercriminals continually find new and inventive ways to exploit unsuspecting individuals. Two such methods that have gained prominence in recent years are smishing (SMS phishing) and vishing (voice phishing). These techniques capitalize on the convenience of modern communication channels, leveraging text messages and voice calls to deceive and manipulate victims. As we navigate the digital age, understanding these threats and adopting preventive measures becomes crucial in safeguarding against scams and frauds. This article delves into the intricacies of smishing and vishing, shedding light on their working mechanisms, potential risks, and strategies to protect oneself.

In an era marked by interconnectedness and digital dependence, the advent of smartphones and mobile communication has revolutionized the way we interact. Alongside these advancements, cybercriminals have found fertile ground to launch sophisticated attacks. Smishing and vishing are prime examples of these attacks, exploiting vulnerabilities in human psychology and communication mediums.

Smishing: Unmasking the Threat

Smishing, a portmanteau of "SMS" and "phishing," refers to the act of sending fraudulent text messages to manipulate individuals into divulging sensitive information or performing malicious actions. Cybercriminals often impersonate legitimate entities, such as banks, government agencies, or service providers, to gain victims' trust and coax them into revealing personal data.

Techniques Employed

Smishing attacks typically employ a variety of techniques to deceive recipients:

1. Spoofed Identities

Attackers utilize techniques to manipulate the sender ID of text messages, making them appear as if they originate from legitimate sources. This adds an air of authenticity to the messages, making recipients more likely to comply.

2. Urgent Appeals

Messages convey a sense of urgency, creating anxiety or fear that compels recipients to act hastily without scrutinizing the message's legitimacy.

3. Tempting Offers

Cybercriminals dangle enticing offers or rewards, luring victims into clicking on malicious links or providing personal information in exchange for supposed benefits.

Risks and Consequences

Falling victim to smishing can have dire consequences:

1. Financial Loss

Victims may unwittingly disclose banking credentials, leading to unauthorized transactions and financial losses.

2. Identity Theft

Personal information shared through smishing can pave the way for identity theft, potentially resulting in long-term repercussions.

3. Malware Infections

Clicking on links in smishing messages can lead to malware infections on smartphones, compromising personal data and device security.

Vishing: The Voice of Deceit

Vishing, or voice phishing, capitalizes on the trust associated with human voice communication to manipulate and deceive individuals. Cybercriminals leverage phone calls to impersonate legitimate entities and extract sensitive information.

1. Call Spoofing

Attackers manipulate caller ID information, making it appear as if calls originate from trustworthy sources. This ploy increases the likelihood of victims complying with the attacker's requests.

2. Manipulative Tactics

Vishing calls often employ emotionally charged tactics, such as impersonating distressed family members or portraying urgent scenarios that pressure victims into divulging information.

3. Impersonating Authority

Attackers may pose as law enforcement officers, government officials, or bank representatives, exploiting victims' trust in authoritative figures.

Safeguarding Against Smishing and Vishing

Protecting oneself from smishing and vishing requires a combination of awareness, vigilance, and preventive measures:

1. Educating Yourself

Familiarize yourself with the tactics employed by cybercriminals in smishing and vishing attacks. Being informed is the first line of defense.

2. Verifying Sources

Before responding to any message or call, independently verify the sender's identity using official contact information from reliable sources.

3. Avoiding Impulsive Actions

Resist the urge to immediately act on urgent or tempting messages or calls. Take time to evaluate the situation and validate the authenticity of the communication.

4. Implementing Security Software

Install reputable security software on your devices to detect and prevent malicious activities, such as malware infections resulting from smishing links.

5. Two-Factor Authentication (2FA)

Enable 2FA for your accounts to add an extra layer of security, making it more challenging for attackers to access your accounts.

6. Reporting Suspicious Activity

Report any suspicious smishing or vishing attempts to relevant authorities, such as your local law enforcement or the Federal Trade Commission (FTC).

Conclusion

In an era defined by rapid technological advancements, smishing and vishing represent contemporary threats that exploit our reliance on mobile communication. By understanding the tactics employed by cybercriminals and adopting proactive measures, individuals can fortify their defenses and navigate the digital landscape with greater confidence. As we continue to embrace the digital age, safeguarding against scams and frauds becomes a collective responsibility, requiring both awareness and action. By staying informed and vigilant, we can mitigate the risks posed by smishing and vishing, ensuring a safer and more secure digital future.

Chapter 5. Fake Social Media Profiles and Catfishing

Introduction

In today's digital age, the internet has revolutionized the way we connect, communicate, and share our lives. Social media platforms have become the epicenter of this online revolution, allowing us to build virtual communities, foster relationships, and express ourselves like never before. However, the same platforms that enable genuine connections have also given rise to a darker side of online interactions – the proliferation of fake social media profiles and the alarming practice of catfishing. Catfishing refers to the act of creating a fake online persona to deceive or manipulate others, often for deceptive or malicious purposes. As we navigate the digital landscape, it becomes imperative to understand the mechanics of these deceptive tactics and equip ourselves with the knowledge to safeguard against scams and frauds.

Anatomy of a Fake Profile

Fake social media profiles are intricately constructed to deceive unsuspecting users. These profiles are often assembled with stolen images, creating a veneer of authenticity. Crafted bios further enhance the illusion, painting a detailed portrait of a fictional individual. To bolster credibility, fake profiles establish a network of friends and followers, creating the appearance of genuine engagement.

Motivations Behind Fake Profiles

The motivations behind these deceptive profiles are varied and often malicious. Financial gain ranks among the top incentives for creating fake profiles. Scammers use these personas to lure individuals into fraudulent schemes, exploiting their trust for monetary advantage. Additionally, fake profiles serve as tools for data mining, enabling the extraction of personal information for further nefarious purposes. In more sinister cases, these profiles can be employed for manipulation and espionage, with social engineering tactics leading to disastrous consequences.

Defining Catfishing

Catfishing, a term that originated from the fishing industry, has now become synonymous with digital deception. It involves creating a fabricated identity to lure unsuspecting individuals into emotional entanglements. The emotional impact of catfishing can be severe, leaving victims grappling with shattered trust, emotional distress, and a sense of betrayal.

Psychological Dynamics of Catfishing

Understanding the motivations behind catfishing is essential to comprehending its intricacies. Catfish often engage in this practice as a form of escapism or fantasy. They seek attention and emotional validation that may be lacking in their own lives. On the other side, victims of catfishing are often vulnerable individuals who are drawn into these deceptive relationships due to their own emotional needs and desires.

Techniques Employed by Catfish

Catfish employ a range of tactics to ensnare their victims. Emotional manipulation is a common strategy, where catfish forge intimate connections through deceitful narratives. Role-playing is another technique, allowing catfish to craft elaborate personas that appeal to their victims' desires. In some cases, catfish engage in the "long con," sustaining the deception over extended periods to deepen emotional ties. A long con, also known as a "big con," is a type of scam where the perpetrator invests an extended duration, often spanning weeks, months, or even longer, in cultivating the victim's trust before ultimately defrauding them.

Recognizing and Safeguarding Against Fake Profiles and Catfishing

Identifying red flags associated with fake profiles is crucial for self-protection. Suspicious profile photos can often be traced back to stolen images through reverse image searching. Inconsistencies in bios and activity should be scrutinized, as these are telltale signs of a fake profile. Limited content and engagement should also raise suspicions.

Building digital resilience is essential to safeguarding against these threats. Educating oneself and others about catfishing can create a community of vigilant users. Protecting personal information is paramount, minimizing the vulnerabilities that catfish exploit. Verifying online connections through independent research and cross-checking can further enhance protection.

In cases where suspicions arise, seeking support and reporting can help mitigate potential harm. Encouraging open conversations about catfishing and related experiences reduces the stigma associated with being a victim. Reporting suspicious activity to platform administrators can result in the removal of fake profiles and catfish. Legal avenues also exist for pursuing action against those who engage in online impersonation.

Case Studies: Real-Life Encounters

1. Megan's Story: A Victim's Account of Falling for a Catfish

Megan's story serves as a cautionary tale of the emotional turmoil and vulnerability that catfishing can inflict upon unsuspecting individuals. It all began innocently enough – a chance encounter on a popular social media platform led Megan to "Alex," a charming and seemingly genuine individual. They exchanged messages that quickly escalated into deep conversations about life, dreams, and shared interests.

Alex's carefully woven narrative portrayed him as the ideal partner Megan had been yearning for. He shared heartwarming stories, provided unwavering emotional support, and made Megan feel cherished in a way she had never experienced before. As their connection deepened, Megan found herself falling in love with the persona Alex had created.

However, doubts started creeping in as inconsistencies emerged in Alex's stories. Megan's friends and family became concerned, pointing out red flags that had eluded her infatuated gaze. With their support, Megan began investigating Alex's background and uncovered a web of deceit. The person she had believed to be Alex was, in fact, a catfish who had used stolen photos and fabricated details to manipulate her emotions.

The revelation shattered Megan's trust and left her grappling with a mix of anger, humiliation, and heartache. Megan's journey towards healing involved seeking therapy to address the emotional scars left by the catfishing experience. Through therapy, she gained insights into the psychology of catfishing and learned valuable lessons about online interactions. Megan now shares her story to raise awareness, advocating for digital resilience and encouraging others to critically evaluate their online relationships.

2. Operation Unmasking: Exposing the Culprit Behind the Mask

"Operation Unmasking" is a powerful testament to the potential impact of collective action against digital deception. In this case, a group of friends united forces to unravel the truth behind a suspicious online persona. It all began when the friends noticed inconsistencies in the behavior of a mutual acquaintance, "Jessie," on social media.

Jessie's online persona had garnered a significant following due to her seemingly adventurous and enviable lifestyle. However, the friends noticed that her stories didn't add up, leading them to suspect that they were dealing with a catfish. Determined to uncover the truth, the group embarked on a meticulously planned investigation.

They employed a combination of techniques, including cross-referencing information, reverse image searching, and analyzing patterns of online activity. As they dug deeper, they discovered that the images Jessie had been using were stolen from various sources, and her online identity was entirely fabricated.

With evidence in hand, the group orchestrated a public awareness campaign to expose the deception. They collaborated on a detailed account of their findings, sharing it across social media platforms frequented by Jessie's followers. The campaign gained traction quickly, sparking discussions about the dangers of catfishing and the importance of verifying online connections.

As a result of their efforts, the catfish was unmasked, and the fake profile was ultimately taken down. The collective action of the group not only protected potential victims from emotional manipulation but also sent a powerful message that digital deception will not go unchecked.

3. Remarks

Megan's story and "Operation Unmasking" shed light on the very real and often devastating consequences of fake social media profiles and catfishing. These cases underscore the need for heightened awareness, critical thinking, and proactive measures when engaging in online relationships. By learning from these experiences, we can equip ourselves with the tools to recognize deception, protect our emotional well-being, and contribute to a safer and more authentic digital landscape. As technology continues to evolve, our vigilance and resilience in the face of digital deception remain paramount.

Conclusion

The prevalence of fake social media profiles and catfishing serves as a sobering reminder that while the digital age offers incredible opportunities for connection, it also exposes us to vulnerabilities that can be exploited by those with ill intent. By understanding the tactics employed by fake profiles and catfish, recognizing the red flags, and actively safeguarding our online interactions, we can reclaim our digital autonomy and ensure that our virtual experiences are characterized by authenticity and trust. As we continue to navigate the evolving digital landscape, the power to unmask deception lies in our hands, empowering us to forge meaningful connections while staying vigilant against scams and frauds.

Introduction

In the modern digital landscape, scams and fraudulent activities have taken on new dimensions, exploiting the vulnerabilities of human emotions. Among these, romance scams have emerged as a particularly insidious form of online deception, capitalizing on the universal desire for companionship and connection. In this article, we delve into the intricate world of romance scams, shedding light on their mechanisms, impact, and, most importantly, strategies to safeguard against them.

The Art of Digital Deception: Anatomy of a Romance Scam

1. The Evolution of Romance Scams

Romance scams have a deep-rooted history that traces back to the pre-digital era. However, the proliferation of the internet and social media has given scammers a powerful platform to exploit unsuspecting individuals. The cloak of anonymity provided by the digital realm allows them to assume false identities and manipulate emotions.

2. Profiling the Scammers: Who Are They?

Romance scammers come from diverse backgrounds and corners of the world. They often operate in organized networks, using scripts and personas to target victims systematically. While some may fit the stereotype of a cunning criminal, others can be seemingly genuine individuals, making detection even more challenging.

3. Luring Victims: The Psychology Behind Romance Scams

Understanding the psychological tactics employed by romance scammers is crucial in comprehending their success. They prey on fundamental human emotions such as loneliness, vulnerability, and the desire for love and affection. By engaging victims in conversations that gradually create emotional dependence, scammers manipulate victims into lowering their guard.

A Tale of False Love: How Romance Scams Unfold

Stage 1: Building Trust and Connection

Romance scams often start innocently, with scammers posing as potential partners on social media or dating platforms. They engage in conversations, asking seemingly harmless questions to gather personal information and understand their victims' vulnerabilities.

Stage 2: Establishing Emotional Intimacy

As conversations progress, scammers skillfully weave intricate narratives, sharing personal stories and experiences to forge a deep emotional bond. Victims begin to feel a sense of connection and trust, making them more susceptible to manipulation.

Stage 3: The Crisis and the Request for Financial Assistance

Once the emotional bond is solidified, scammers engineer a crisis that requires urgent financial intervention. This could be a medical emergency, a business setback, or a personal tragedy. Victims, caught in a web of emotional investment, are more likely to comply with the scammer's requests for financial assistance.

The Toll of Deception: Emotional and Financial Impact

1. Psychological Trauma on Victims

The aftermath of a romance scam is emotionally devastating for victims. The realization that a deep emotional connection was based on lies can lead to feelings of betrayal, shame, and humiliation. Victims often struggle with trust issues, making it challenging to engage in future relationships.

2. Financial Losses: From Hearts to Hard-Earned Money

Beyond the emotional toll, romance scams also lead to significant financial losses. Victims may end up sending large sums of money to scammers, depleting their savings and incurring debts. The financial consequences can be long-lasting, affecting victims' financial stability and well-being.

The Digital Armor: Safeguarding Against Romance Scams

1. Educating for Awareness: Recognizing the Red Flags

To protect oneself from romance scams, awareness is key. Educating individuals about common red flags can help them identify potential scams. Inconsistencies in stories, requests for financial assistance, hasty declarations of love, and reluctance to share personal information are all warning signs that should not be ignored.

Verifying the identities and intentions of online connections is a crucial step in avoiding romance scams. Conducting reverse image searches, cross-checking information with social media profiles, and seeking advice from trusted friends or family members can provide valuable insights into the authenticity of an online relationship.

Preventive measures play a vital role in safeguarding against romance scams. Setting strict privacy settings on social media, limiting the sharing of personal information, and using secure and reputable dating platforms can help reduce the risk of falling victim to scams.

In the unfortunate event of falling victim to a romance scam, taking immediate action is essential. Contacting law enforcement and relevant authorities, reporting the scam to online platforms, and seeking support from anti-scam organizations can aid in pursuing legal action and recovering from the emotional aftermath.

Building Digital Resilience: Navigating the Complexities of Online Relationships

While romance scams highlight the risks of online relationships, it's important not to let fear overshadow the potential for genuine connections. Balancing caution with openness can help individuals navigate the complexities of the digital world more effectively.

2. Fostering Genuine Connections: Honesty and Authenticity

In the pursuit of meaningful online relationships, honesty and authenticity are paramount. Being genuine about intentions, sharing accurate information, and respecting boundaries can foster connections built on trust and mutual respect.

3. Nurturing Healthy Skepticism: Embracing Online Dating Safely

Approaching online dating with healthy skepticism is an essential aspect of safeguarding against romance scams. Engaging in open conversations about online safety, encouraging critical thinking, and staying informed about the latest scam tactics can empower individuals to make informed decisions.

Conclusion

As the digital era continues to reshape the way we connect and communicate, the threat of romance scams reminds us of the darker side of this technological advancement. By unraveling the complexities of romance scams and equipping individuals with knowledge, vigilance, and digital resilience, we can forge meaningful connections while safeguarding against the deceptive tactics of those who seek to exploit our emotions and trust. In a world where genuine love and companionship are prized, it's imperative to remain cautious, yet hopeful, in the pursuit of digital relationships.

Introduction

In an era dominated by advanced technology and unprecedented connectivity, the digital landscape has paved the way for both remarkable innovation and alarming vulnerabilities. One such alarming phenomenon that has gained significant attention is the rise of AI-generated fake content, commonly known as deepfakes. These seemingly innocuous creations harbor the potential to undermine truth, manipulate public opinion, and facilitate scams and frauds. In this article, we delve into the world of deepfakes, exploring their implications, challenges, and potential safeguards within the context of safeguarding against scams and frauds in the digital age.

The Evolution of Digital Deception

The term "deepfake" originates from the amalgamation of "deep learning" and "fake." It refers to the use of artificial intelligence, particularly deep learning algorithms, to create hyper-realistic, fabricated content, often involving manipulating visual, auditory, or textual information. While the technology's genesis lies in harmless pursuits like entertainment and creative expression, it has rapidly spiraled into a realm of nefarious applications.

The Diverse Landscape of Deepfakes

Deepfakes encompass a wide range of deceptive content types, each possessing its unique set of challenges and risks:

1. Visual Deception: Manipulating Faces and Expressions

Deepfake technology can convincingly replace an individual's face in a video or image, rendering them capable of saying and doing things they never actually did. This visual deception has serious implications for identity theft, revenge pornography, and political misinformation.

2. Audio Manipulation: Crafting Synthetic Voices

AI-generated voices can replicate an individual's speech patterns and tone with astonishing accuracy. Cybercriminals can use this technology to impersonate someone and commit fraud through voice-based scams.

3. Textual Deception: Crafting Synthetic Text

Advanced language models can generate written content that closely mimics an individual's writing style. This poses threats to the authenticity of written communication, enabling scammers to impersonate individuals and deceive their targets.

Implications for Scams and Frauds

The proliferation of deepfake technology has ushered in a new era of scams and frauds that exploit its deceptive capabilities:

1. Business Email Compromise (BEC) Scams

Deepfakes can mimic an executive's voice, facilitating BEC scams where employees are tricked into transferring funds based on fraudulent voice commands.

2. Impersonation Frauds

Fraudsters can impersonate family members, colleagues, or financial institutions through convincing deepfake videos or audios to solicit money or sensitive information.

3. Misinformation and Social Engineering

Deepfakes can be weaponized for political misinformation, sowing discord, and manipulating public opinion, thereby exacerbating the challenges of fake news and disinformation campaigns.

Challenges in Detection and Mitigation

Combatting the menace of AI-generated fake content is a multifaceted challenge:

1. Technological Advancements Outpacing Detection Tools

As deepfake technology evolves, detecting these fabricated pieces becomes progressively challenging. Traditional methods of identifying digital manipulations are often rendered ineffective.

2. Vast Data Availability and Training

The abundance of publicly available data contributes to the training of AI models that power deepfakes, making it easier to create convincing forgeries.

3. Privacy Concerns

The potential misuse of deepfake technology raises serious privacy concerns, as individuals' likenesses and voices can be exploited without consent.

Safeguarding Against Deepfake-Driven Scams

While the battle against deepfake-driven scams and frauds is ongoing, several strategies can be employed to safeguard against their malicious impact:

1. Educational Initiatives

Raising awareness about deepfake technology and its potential applications can empower individuals to be cautious and discerning consumers of digital content.

2. Advanced Authentication Mechanisms

Implementing multifactor authentication and voice biometrics can add an extra layer of security against voice-based scams.

3. Digital Content Watermarking

Embedding tamper-evident watermarks in images and videos can help verify the authenticity of visual content.

4. Blockchain Technology

Leveraging blockchain's immutable nature can aid in verifying the source and authenticity of digital content, mitigating the risk of misinformation.

Legal and Ethical Considerations

The legal and ethical implications of deepfakes are complex and multifaceted:

1. Regulation and Legislation

Governments and tech companies must collaborate to develop comprehensive regulations that address the creation, distribution, and use of deepfakes.

2. Digital Signature and Consent

Introducing mechanisms for obtaining digital consent or signatures for the use of an individual's likeness in AI-generated content can mitigate potential abuses.

The Way Forward: A Collaborative Approach

Safeguarding against scams and frauds in the digital age necessitates a concerted effort from individuals, governments, and technology developers:

1. Continuous Technological Innovation

Developing advanced AI algorithms and tools for detecting and combating deepfakes is essential to stay ahead of malicious actors.

2. Media Literacy and Critical Thinking

Promoting media literacy and critical thinking skills can empower individuals to critically evaluate the content they consume.

3. Global Cooperation

International collaboration is pivotal in establishing norms, standards, and regulations that address the cross-border nature of deepfake-driven scams.

Conclusion: Navigating the Digital Quagmire

AI-generated fake content, in the form of deepfakes, presents a multifaceted challenge that demands vigilance, innovation, and global collaboration. As the digital landscape continues to evolve, the risks associated with deepfakes underscore the urgency of fortifying our defenses against scams and frauds. By fostering a culture of skepticism, embracing advanced technologies, and advocating for ethical and regulatory frameworks, we can aspire to navigate the complex labyrinth of AI-generated deception and emerge as resilient custodians of truth in the digital age.

Introduction

In an era characterized by rapid technological advancement and digitization, the convenience and efficiency offered by artificial intelligence (AI) are undeniable. Chatbots, AI-powered virtual assistants designed to engage in human-like conversations, have become an integral part of our digital landscape. Chatbots are AI-powered computer programs designed to simulate human conversation and provide automated responses in chat interfaces. Robocalls are automated phone calls that deliver pre-recorded messages, often used for telemarketing or informational purposes. However, with the rise of AI, there has also been an alarming increase in chatbot scams and AI-driven robocalls, exploiting the very technology meant to enhance our lives. This article explores the intricate web of deception woven by scammers, the tactics they employ, and the measures individuals can take to safeguard themselves against these evolving threats.

The Digital Frontier of Deception

As our world becomes increasingly interconnected through the digital realm, scammers and fraudsters find innovative ways to exploit emerging technologies for their gain. Chatbots, originally designed to streamline customer service and offer personalized experiences, have been subverted by malicious actors to manipulate, deceive, and extort unsuspecting victims.

The Anatomy of Chatbot Scams

1. Impersonation and Social Engineering: Chatbot scammers often impersonate trusted entities such as banks, government agencies, or popular brands. They prey on individuals' trust, using sophisticated social engineering techniques to manipulate emotions and elicit sensitive information.

2. Phishing and Spoofing: Through AI-driven interactions, scammers mimic legitimate communication, sending links to malicious websites or asking for login credentials under the guise of routine procedures. Unsuspecting users, unaware of the trap, willingly divulge confidential information.

3. Fake Promotions and Giveaways: Chatbots lure victims with irresistible offers, fake discounts, and promises of lucrative prizes. These ploys encourage individuals to share personal data or make monetary transactions, ultimately falling into the scammer's trap.

The Rise of AI-Driven Robocalls

1. Automated Voice Impersonation: AI-driven robocalls employ voice synthesis technology to convincingly mimic trusted figures, such as family members or company executives. This manipulation aims to deceive recipients into complying with fraudulent requests.

2. Investment Scams and Financial Manipulation: Scammers exploit AI to conduct large-scale robocall campaigns, promoting fraudulent investment opportunities or coercing victims into transferring funds to fictitious accounts.

3. Healthcare and Insurance Fraud: AI-driven robocalls exploit individuals' concerns about health and insurance matters, offering fake policies, medical products, or services. These scams prey on vulnerability and desperation.

Unraveling the Web: How Scammers Exploit AI

1. Machine Learning and Natural Language Processing: Scammers leverage AI's capabilities in machine learning and natural language processing to create chatbots that can engage in seemingly authentic conversations, making it difficult to distinguish them from genuine interactions.

2. Data Harvesting and Profiling: AI-powered chatbots engage users in extended dialogues, extracting personal information to build detailed profiles. This data is then weaponized for targeted scams or sold on the dark web.

3. Adaptive Scam Tactics: AI allows scammers to continuously refine their tactics based on user responses, making their approaches more sophisticated and adaptive. This dynamic behavior complicates detection and prevention efforts.

Safeguarding Against AI-Driven Deception

1. Education and Awareness: Raising public awareness about the existence and intricacies of chatbot scams and AI-driven robocalls is crucial. Knowledge empowers individuals to recognize red flags and exercise caution.

2. Verification Protocols: Implementing multi-step verification processes and cross-referencing information can add an extra layer of security, ensuring that interactions

are genuine and minimizing the risk of falling victim to scams.

3. AI-Powered Detection: Just as AI is used by scammers, it can also be harnessed by cybersecurity professionals to develop advanced detection algorithms capable of identifying suspicious patterns and behaviors in real-time.

4. Robocall Blockers and Filters: Utilizing AI-driven tools that identify and block robocalls can significantly reduce exposure to fraudulent schemes, providing a defense mechanism against unwanted and potentially harmful interactions.

The Ethical Implications of AI in Scams

1. Algorithmic Responsibility: As AI becomes more entrenched in scams and fraud, questions arise about the ethical responsibilities of AI developers and providers in combatting these threats and preventing misuse.

2. Privacy Concerns: The collection and exploitation of personal data by scammers raise concerns about individual privacy rights. Striking a balance between AI's potential and safeguarding personal information becomes imperative.

Conclusion: Navigating the Future of Digital Deception

In a digital age marked by both innovation and exploitation, the battle against chatbot scams and AI-driven robocalls is an ongoing one. The inherent power of AI to mimic human interaction, combined with malicious intent, creates a complex landscape of deception. By fostering awareness, leveraging advanced AI technologies for detection and prevention, and promoting ethical considerations, individuals and societies can fortify themselves against the evolving tide of digital scams, ensuring that the promise of AI remains a force for good rather than a tool of deception.

Chapter 9. AI-Powered Phishing and Social Engineering with AI

Introduction

In today's digital age, the rapid advancement of technology has brought both unprecedented convenience and unforeseen challenges. One such challenge is the proliferation of scams and frauds, with phishing and social engineering being two of the most prevalent and insidious threats. As if these threats weren't formidable enough on their own, the emergence of AI-powered tools and techniques has taken these tactics to a whole new level of sophistication and danger.

As technology evolves, so do the strategies employed by cybercriminals. Traditional phishing and social engineering techniques have relied on exploiting human psychology and vulnerabilities. However, the integration of artificial intelligence into these malicious activities has given rise to a new breed of threats that are more convincing, adaptive, and difficult to detect.

The Evolution of Phishing and Social Engineering

Phishing and social engineering have a long history, dating back to the early days of the internet. These tactics involve manipulating individuals into divulging sensitive information, such as passwords, financial details, or personal data. Initially, attackers relied on basic email scams and deceptive websites. Over time, these attacks became more sophisticated, targeting specific individuals and organizations.

The Role of AI in Phishing and Social Engineering

The advent of AI has transformed the threat landscape. AI-powered phishing and social engineering attacks leverage machine learning algorithms and natural language processing to craft highly personalized and convincing messages. These messages are designed to exploit the recipient's emotions, preferences, and behaviors, making them more likely to fall victim.

Advanced Personalization Techniques

AI allows attackers to gather and analyze vast amounts of data from social media, public records, and other sources. This data is then used to create highly personalized messages that appear legitimate and trustworthy. Attackers can mimic the writing style of the target, reference recent events, and even imitate the communication patterns of known contacts.

Deepfake Technology and Voice Cloning

Deepfake technology enables the creation of highly realistic audio and video content. Attackers can use voice cloning to impersonate trusted individuals, such as colleagues, family members, or even company executives. These manipulated recordings can be used to make urgent requests for sensitive information or financial transactions, exploiting the victim's trust.

Automated Spear Phishing

AI-powered tools can automate the process of identifying and targeting potential victims. By analyzing publicly available information, attackers can identify high-value targets and tailor their messages accordingly. This automated spear-phishing approach increases the efficiency and success rate of attacks.

Evading Detection with AI

AI is not only used for crafting convincing messages but also for evading detection by security systems. Attackers can use AI algorithms to generate variations of malicious content, making it challenging for traditional security measures to keep up. This cat-and-mouse game between attackers and defenders emphasizes the need for adaptive cybersecurity solutions.

Psychological Manipulation and Emotional Exploitation

AI-powered attacks capitalize on human psychology and emotions. These attacks are designed to evoke strong emotional responses, such as fear, urgency, or curiosity. By manipulating emotions, attackers increase the likelihood that victims will make impulsive decisions without critically evaluating the legitimacy of the request.

Combating AI-Powered Threats

Safeguarding against AI-powered phishing and social engineering requires a multi-faceted approach that combines technological solutions with education and awareness. Some strategies include:

1. Advanced Email Filters: Employing AI-driven email filters can help detect and block phishing attempts by analyzing message content, sender behavior, and context.

2. Behavioral Analysis: Monitoring user behavior for unusual patterns can help identify potential attacks, as AI

algorithms can learn to recognize deviations from normal activities.

3. User Education: Educating individuals about the dangers of AI-powered attacks and encouraging skepticism when receiving unsolicited requests can significantly reduce the success of such attacks.

4. Multi-Factor Authentication (MFA): Implementing MFA adds an extra layer of security, making it harder for attackers to access sensitive accounts even if they have obtained some credentials.

5. AI-Powered Defense: Employing AI-driven cybersecurity solutions that adapt and learn from emerging threats can help organizations stay ahead of attackers.

The Future of AI-Powered Phishing and Social Engineering

As AI technology continues to advance, so too will the tactics used by cybercriminals. The future may see even more convincing deepfake content, more sophisticated automated attacks, and increased targeting of AI-generated synthetic identities. Staying vigilant and continuously improving cybersecurity measures will be paramount to mitigating these evolving threats.

Conclusion

AI-powered phishing and social engineering represent a formidable challenge in the digital age. The convergence of AI and cybercrime has led to more personalized, convincing, and dangerous attacks. Organizations and individuals must remain vigilant, adapt their defenses, and prioritize education and awareness to safeguard against these evolving threats. As technology progresses, so too must our efforts to protect ourselves from the ever-evolving landscape of scams and frauds.

Chapter 10. AI-Enhanced Business Email Compromise (BEC)

Introduction

In an era dominated by digital innovation, the landscape of scams and frauds has evolved exponentially, raising the need for robust countermeasures to safeguard individuals and businesses alike. Among the plethora of cyber threats, Business Email Compromise (BEC) has emerged as a particularly potent form of deception, with its capabilities further amplified by the integration of artificial intelligence (AI). This article delves into the intricate realm of AI-Enhanced BEC, exploring its nuances, implications, and strategies for mitigation within the overarching theme of "Safeguarding Against Scams and Frauds in the Digital Age."

The Rise of BEC and AI

The digital age has brought unprecedented convenience and efficiency to the business world, but it has also exposed vulnerabilities that malicious actors are quick to exploit. Business Email Compromise, a sophisticated form of cybercrime, involves manipulating individuals into transferring funds or sensitive information under the guise of legitimate requests. This fraudulent practice has seen a significant surge in recent years, propelled by the proliferation of digital communication channels and the ever-increasing reliance on electronic transactions.

As technology evolves, so do the methods of attackers. Enter Artificial Intelligence, the game-changer that has revolutionized numerous industries. AI's integration into cybercrime techniques has given rise to AI-Enhanced BEC, a more cunning and convincing iteration of traditional BEC schemes.

The Mechanics of AI-Enhanced BEC

1. Precise Targeting through Data Mining

AI-Enhanced BEC starts with data mining, where attackers leverage AI algorithms to gather comprehensive information about potential victims. This may include email histories, social media profiles, and corporate structures. By analyzing this data, attackers can pinpoint key individuals within organizations and craft highly personalized, convincing messages.

2. Spear Phishing Refined

Spear phishing lies at the core of BEC attacks. AI introduces a new level of sophistication, allowing attackers to create emails that mirror the writing style of the target. This not only lends an air of authenticity but also evades conventional email security filters.

3. Contextual Awareness and Realism

AI-Enhanced BEC emails are designed to reflect the target's work environment and ongoing projects. They incorporate accurate details, such as upcoming events, current negotiations, or recent transactions. This contextual awareness enhances the illusion of legitimacy and increases the likelihood of success.

AI's Role in Evasion and Manipulation

1. Evasion of Detection Mechanisms

AI-powered attacks possess the capability to adapt and modify their tactics in real-time. This evasion strategy thwarts traditional email security systems, which often rely on predefined patterns to flag suspicious emails. The dynamic nature of AI-Enhanced BEC makes it a formidable adversary in the realm of cyber defense.

2. Psychological Manipulation

AI-Enhanced BEC leverages psychological manipulation techniques to exploit human psychology. By analyzing communication patterns, AI can determine the optimal time to strike, crafting emails that capitalize on moments of vulnerability or urgency.

Consequences and Case Studies

1. Financial Losses and Reputational Damage

The aftermath of a successful AI-Enhanced BEC attack is marked by severe financial losses and lasting reputational damage. The funds diverted from legitimate channels disrupt business operations and can lead to cascading financial implications.

2. Case Study: The AI-Enhanced CEO Fraud

In the annals of cybercrime, the AI-Enhanced CEO Fraud stands out as a chilling demonstration of how cutting-edge technology can be harnessed for malicious intent. This case study serves as a stark reminder of the unprecedented sophistication that AI brings to traditional scams, revealing the extent to which attackers can manipulate and exploit human psychology for financial gain.

The Setting: A Multinational Corporation

The target of this audacious attack was a prominent multinational corporation, renowned for its expansive global operations and financial prowess. The organization's CEO was a well-respected figure in the business world, commanding a high level of authority and recognition within the company. With extensive financial dealings taking place across international borders, the corporation presented an enticing opportunity for cybercriminals seeking to capitalize on its intricate financial web.

The Intricate Planning Phase

The perpetrators embarked on a meticulous planning phase, leveraging AI technologies to gather detailed information about the target company, its organizational structure, and the CEO's communication patterns. Advanced AI algorithms scoured public sources, corporate websites, and social media platforms to amass a treasure trove of data, meticulously mapping out the company's hierarchy, ongoing projects, and even the CEO's linguistic idiosyncrasies.

This wealth of information allowed the attackers to replicate the CEO's communication style with uncanny precision. They meticulously crafted a fraudulent email that mirrored the CEO's writing tone and addressed an unsuspecting employee by name. The email exploited the familiarity and authority associated with the CEO, setting the stage for a sophisticated ruse.

The AI-Enhanced Deception

Where this attack truly showcased the power of AI was in its execution. The attackers employed AI-generated voice technology to create a voice recording that strikingly resembled the CEO's vocal patterns and intonation. The email contained a directive for the recipient, a mid-level manager responsible for financial transactions, to urgently transfer a substantial sum of money to a designated offshore account. The email was timed to coincide with a critical phase of ongoing negotiations, adding an element of urgency and heightened emotional stress.

The email's content was tailored to align with the company's ongoing projects, making reference to sensitive details and negotiations that only a high-ranking executive like the CEO would possess. This meticulous attention to context and relevance further reinforced the email's authenticity.

The Perilous Success and Subsequent Fallout

Trapped within a web of convincing deception, the mid-level manager complied with the CEO's apparent request. The substantial sum was transferred to the offshore account as instructed, unbeknownst to the organization's leadership. The attackers successfully bypassed traditional security measures and overcame the manager's initial skepticism through a combination of AI-generated content, personalization, and expert timing.

The fallout was swift and severe. The unauthorized transfer went unnoticed until several days later, by which time the funds had been irretrievably funneled into untraceable accounts. The financial loss reverberated through the corporation, causing disruptions to ongoing projects, tarnishing the company's reputation, and triggering a scramble to address the breach.

Lessons Learned and Countermeasures

The AI-Enhanced CEO Fraud case study underscores the imperative of vigilance and comprehensive cybersecurity measures in the face of evolving threats. The following lessons and countermeasures emerge from this chilling scenario:

Heightened Employee Training: The incident highlights the need for ongoing employee training to ensure that individuals are equipped to identify and respond to unusual or suspicious requests, even when they appear to originate from high-ranking executives.

Multi-Factor Verification: Introducing multi-factor verification processes for financial transactions and critical communications can add an extra layer of security, making it more difficult for attackers to succeed.

AI-Powered Authentication: Organizations can consider integrating AI-powered authentication systems that analyze communication patterns and vocal characteristics to verify the authenticity of high-stakes requests.

Robust Email Monitoring: Employing advanced AI-driven email monitoring solutions can help detect anomalies, flagging potentially fraudulent communications for closer scrutiny.

Incident Response Plans: Developing comprehensive incident response plans that outline immediate actions to be taken in the event of a suspected breach can minimize the impact of a successful attack.

The AI-Enhanced CEO Fraud case study stands as a stark testament to the evolving nature of cybercrime, underscoring the imperative for organizations to adapt and fortify their defenses against the ever-shifting landscape of digital deception. By harnessing the power of AI for both offense and defense, businesses can strive to stay one step ahead in the ongoing battle against sophisticated cyber threats.

Mitigation and Prevention Strategies

1. Enhanced Email Security

Organizations must invest in advanced email security solutions that incorporate AI algorithms to detect and counteract AI-Enhanced BEC attacks. These solutions can identify anomalies in communication patterns and linguistic nuances, helping distinguish genuine emails from fraudulent ones.

2. Employee Training and Awareness

Educating employees about the intricacies of AI-Enhanced BEC attacks is pivotal. Regular training sessions can familiarize staff with potential red flags, equipping them to identify suspicious communication and respond appropriately.

3. Two-Factor Authentication (2FA) and Verification Protocols

Incorporating multi-factor authentication and verification protocols for financial transactions and sensitive communications can serve as an additional layer of defense against AI-Enhanced BEC attacks.

The battle against AI-Enhanced BEC can leverage AI itself. Organizations can employ AI-powered tools that analyze communication patterns and flag potential threats, effectively staying one step ahead of cybercriminals.

Conclusion

As technology continues to advance, the threat landscape of cybercrime will inevitably evolve alongside it. AI-Enhanced Business Email Compromise represents a formidable challenge, pushing the boundaries of deception and manipulation. In the face of this threat, a proactive and multidimensional approach is imperative. By embracing advanced security measures, prioritizing employee education, and harnessing the power of AI for defense, organizations can fortify themselves against the insidious realm of AI-Enhanced BEC, ultimately safeguarding their interests in the complex and interconnected digital age.

Introduction

In today's interconnected world, where technology permeates every facet of our lives, the digital landscape offers unparalleled convenience and opportunities. However, this technological advancement also brings with it a darker side – an increase in scams and fraudulent activities that prey on unsuspecting individuals. Among these, tech support scams and fake apps have emerged as potent threats, exploiting users' trust and vulnerabilities for financial gain. This article explores the intricate web of deception woven by these scams, shedding light on their mechanics, impact, and most importantly, strategies to safeguard against them.

Understanding Tech Support Scams

Tech support scams are a sophisticated form of deception that manipulate users into believing they have encountered a serious computer problem. Perpetrators impersonate legitimate tech support agents, often utilizing convincing scripts, pop-up messages, and even cold calls to create a sense of urgency and anxiety. The subterfuge is intended to prompt victims to grant remote access to their devices or divulge sensitive information, thereby granting the scammer control over the victim's system or personal data.

Tactics Employed by Tech Support Scammers

1. Impersonation and Social Engineering: Scammers often pose as representatives from reputable tech companies,

exploiting the trust users place in these entities. They use a variety of tactics to appear legitimate, including spoofed caller IDs, official-sounding email addresses, and even hijacked websites.

2. Pop-Up Alarms and Fake Error Messages: Malicious websites or pop-ups display alarming messages about system errors or virus infections, coercing users into contacting the supposed tech support number provided.

3. Fear and Urgency: Scammers manipulate emotions by creating a sense of urgency. Victims are told that unless immediate action is taken, their data will be compromised or their devices irreparably damaged.

The Impact of Tech Support Scams

The consequences of falling victim to tech support scams can be dire, both financially and emotionally.

1. Financial Loss: Scammers often demand payment for "fixing" nonexistent issues or offer bogus software subscriptions. Victims may also be coerced into purchasing unnecessary services or software.

2. Identity Theft: Sharing personal and financial information with scammers can lead to identity theft and financial fraud, causing long-term damage to victims' credit and reputation.

3. Loss of Data: Granting remote access can result in the installation of malicious software, leading to the loss of important data and even complete system compromise.

Fake Apps: Unmasking the Digital Deception

Fake apps are another insidious form of digital deception that exploit users' reliance on mobile applications for various tasks. These fraudulent applications impersonate legitimate ones, often with the goal of stealing sensitive information or spreading malware.

The Anatomy of Fake Apps

1. App Store Impersonation: Scammers create fake apps that closely resemble popular and trusted applications. These counterfeits often have similar icons, names, and user interfaces, making them difficult to distinguish from the genuine versions.

2. Malicious Code Injection: Some fake apps contain hidden malicious code that can compromise the user's device, steal personal data, or perform unauthorized actions.

3. Data Harvesting: Fraudulent apps may request excessive permissions, granting them access to sensitive data, such as contacts, location, and messages. This information can then be exploited for various purposes, including targeted phishing attacks.

Protecting Against Tech Support Scams and Fake Apps

Preventing falling victim to tech support scams and fake apps requires a combination of vigilance, education, and proactive measures.

1. Stay Informed: Educate yourself and your loved ones about common scams, warning signs, and tactics employed by scammers. Knowledge is the first line of defense.

2. Verify Legitimacy: If you receive unsolicited tech support calls or messages, independently verify the identity of the caller or sender by contacting the official company through their verified channels.

3. Use Official Channels: Download apps only from official app stores like the Apple App Store or Google Play Store. Avoid third-party app sources, as they are more prone to hosting fake apps.

4. Check Reviews and Ratings: Before downloading any app, check its reviews and ratings. Be wary of apps with few reviews or overwhelmingly positive feedback, as they might be fake.

5. Review Permissions: Scrutinize the permissions an app requests before installation. If an app asks for unnecessary access, reconsider installing it.

6. Keep Software Updated: Regularly update your operating system, applications, and security software to patch vulnerabilities that scammers might exploit.

Conclusion

Tech support scams and fake apps represent a growing menace in the digital age, exploiting users' trust and vulnerabilities for financial gain. However, armed with knowledge and a cautious approach, individuals can protect themselves against these sophisticated scams. By staying informed, verifying legitimacy, and exercising vigilance, we can navigate the digital landscape with confidence, safeguarding ourselves and our loved ones from the perils of online deception.

Chapter 12. Online Auction Fraud and AI-Driven Online Auction Fraud

Introduction

The rapid advancement of technology and the proliferation of online platforms have revolutionized the way we conduct business and interact with the world. Online auctions, in particular, have gained significant popularity, providing a convenient platform for buying and selling a wide range of items. However, with the rise of online auctions, there has also been an alarming increase in fraudulent activities, leading to significant financial losses for unsuspecting victims. This article delves into the world of online auction fraud, its various forms, and the role of artificial intelligence (AI) in both perpetrating and preventing these scams.

Understanding Online Auction Fraud

Online auction fraud, commonly referred to as auction scams, encompasses a range of deceptive practices where criminals exploit the anonymity and lack of face-to-face interaction inherent in online auctions. This section explores some of the most prevalent types of online auction fraud:

1. Misrepresentation of Goods: Fraudsters may exaggerate the condition, value, or authenticity of an item to attract higher bids. This can include posting misleading images, providing false descriptions, or even selling counterfeit goods.

2. Non-Delivery Scams: In this scheme, the scammer receives payment for an item but fails to deliver it, leaving the buyer with an empty wallet and no merchandise.

3. Shill Bidding: Criminals engage in shill bidding by creating fake accounts or enlisting accomplices to place fake bids on their own items. This artificially inflates the bidding price and coerces legitimate buyers into bidding more.

4. Bid Siphoning: Scammers may approach legitimate sellers with an offer to purchase an item outside the auction platform, diverting potential buyers away from the auction and leaving the seller with no final sale.

5. Phishing and Identity Theft: Fraudsters use fake websites or emails that mimic legitimate auction platforms to steal users' personal and financial information, leading to unauthorized access to accounts or financial losses.

Safeguarding Against Online Auction Fraud

As online auction fraud continues to threaten the integrity of digital marketplaces, individuals and platforms alike must implement robust measures to safeguard against these scams:

1. User Education: Educating users about the common tactics used in online auction fraud, such as misrepresentation and non-delivery, can empower them to make informed decisions and avoid falling victim to scams.

2. Verification and Reputation Systems: Auction platforms can implement verification processes for sellers, ensuring their legitimacy and providing buyers with a higher level of

confidence. Additionally, reputation systems can help users identify trustworthy sellers based on past transactions.

3. Secure Payment Gateways: Implementing secure and trusted payment gateways can protect both buyers and sellers from unauthorized transactions and non-delivery scams.

4. Transparent Feedback Mechanisms: Platforms should encourage users to provide honest feedback and reviews after transactions, helping to establish a transparent and accountable marketplace.

5. Escrow Services: Introducing escrow services can ensure that payment is held by a third party until the buyer receives the purchased item, reducing the risk of non-delivery scams.

AI-Driven Online Auction Fraud

As technology evolves, fraudsters are leveraging AI to devise more sophisticated and convincing scams. AI-driven online auction fraud introduces new challenges and complexities, as well as potential solutions. Several ways AI is used in perpetrating fraud include:

1. Automated Scam Creation: AI-powered tools can generate convincing item descriptions and images, making it easier for scammers to mislead potential buyers.

2. Dynamic Pricing Manipulation: Fraudsters can use AI algorithms to dynamically adjust prices based on user behaviors and market trends, luring buyers into bidding higher.

3. Advanced Shill Bidding: AI-driven bots can mimic human behavior and engage in shill bidding, making it harder to distinguish fraudulent activities from legitimate bids.

4. Personalized Phishing Attacks: AI can analyze user data to craft highly personalized phishing messages, increasing the likelihood of victims falling for these scams.

Safeguarding Against AI-Driven Online Auction Fraud

While AI contributes to the evolution of online auction fraud, it also offers powerful tools to counter these scams:

1. AI-Powered Detection Algorithms: Auction platforms can employ AI algorithms to analyze user behaviors, flag suspicious activities, and identify potential fraudsters.

2. Natural Language Processing (NLP): NLP algorithms can scrutinize item descriptions for inconsistencies or misleading language, alerting users to potential scams.

3. User Behavior Analysis: AI can detect unusual bidding patterns or account behaviors, helping to identify both fraudulent buyers and sellers.

4. Image Analysis: AI-driven image recognition can verify the authenticity of items by comparing images to a database of known counterfeit goods.

5. Multi-Factor Authentication: AI-based multi-factor authentication can add an extra layer of security to prevent unauthorized access to accounts.

Conclusion

As online auction platforms continue to thrive, the threat of fraud looms large. Understanding the various forms of online auction fraud and the role of AI in facilitating and preventing these scams is essential for both users and platform operators. While AI-driven fraud presents new challenges, it also offers innovative solutions that can be harnessed to protect users and maintain the integrity of online auctions in the digital age. As technology evolves, so too must our strategies to safeguard against scams and frauds, ensuring a secure and trustworthy online marketplace for all.

Introduction

In the digital age, where technology has revolutionized communication and interaction, the threat of scams and frauds has also evolved to exploit unsuspecting individuals. One prevalent form of deception that has gained prominence is lottery and prize scams. These schemes lure victims with promises of large sums of money or valuable prizes, exploiting their hopes and dreams. In this article, we delve into the world of lottery and prize scams, exploring their tactics, red flags, and effective strategies to safeguard against falling victim to these malicious schemes.

Understanding Lottery and Prize Scams

Lottery and prize scams entail a deceptive ploy in which fraudsters contact individuals, typically through email, phone calls, or social media, claiming that the recipient has won a significant sum of money or a valuable prize. The scammers often use fabricated stories and official-sounding language to create a sense of credibility and urgency, leading victims to believe they must take immediate action to claim their winnings.

Tactics Employed by Scammers

1. Impersonating Legitimate Organizations: Scammers frequently pose as representatives of legitimate lotteries, sweepstakes, or well-known companies to create a sense of legitimacy. They may even use official logos and documentation to make their claims appear authentic.

2. Urgency and Pressure: Scammers play on victims' emotions by creating a sense of urgency, insisting that immediate action is required to claim the prize. They may use tactics like time-sensitive deadlines or threats of forfeiting the winnings to manipulate victims into complying.

3. Advance Fee Payment: One of the most common tactics involves requesting victims to pay fees, taxes, or administrative charges upfront in order to release their supposed winnings. Once the victim pays, the scammer disappears, leaving the victim with financial losses.

4. Personal Information Harvesting: Scammers often ask for personal and financial information under the guise of verifying the recipient's identity. This information can be used for identity theft and other fraudulent activities.

Red Flags to Watch Out For

1. Unsolicited Notifications: Legitimate lotteries and sweepstakes do not contact winners out of the blue. Be wary of unsolicited emails, phone calls, or social media messages claiming you've won a prize.

2. Requests for Payments: Any request for upfront payments or fees to claim a prize is a clear warning sign of a scam. Legitimate winnings do not require payment to release.

3. Poor Grammar and Spelling: Scammers often originate from regions where English is not the primary language, resulting in poorly written messages riddled with grammar and spelling errors.

4. Too Good to Be True: If an offer seems too good to be true, it likely is. Be skeptical of large sums of money or prizes that you never entered to win.

5. Lack of Official Documentation: Legitimate lotteries provide official documentation outlining the terms and conditions of the prize. Lack of such documentation is a red flag.

Safeguarding Against Lottery and Prize Scams

1. Verify the Source: Independently research the organization or company claiming to offer the prize. Contact them directly using official contact information to confirm the legitimacy of the claim.

2. Don't Share Personal Information: Avoid sharing personal, financial, or sensitive information with unknown individuals or organizations. Legitimate prize providers will not require such information upfront.

3. Question and Investigate: Ask questions and seek detailed information about the prize, including how you were selected as a winner and the process for claiming the prize.

4. Resist Pressure: Scammers often use high-pressure tactics to rush victims into making decisions. Take your time, and don't be swayed by urgency.

5. Educate Yourself: Stay informed about common scams and frauds. Familiarize yourself with the tactics scammers use so you can recognize potential threats.

Reporting Scams

If you suspect you have encountered a lottery or prize scam, report it to the appropriate authorities, such as the Federal Trade Commission (FTC) in the United States or the relevant consumer protection agency in your country. Reporting scams helps authorities track and take action against fraudsters.

Conclusion

Lottery and prize scams are a grave concern in the digital age, preying on individuals' aspirations and vulnerabilities. By understanding the tactics scammers employ and staying vigilant, you can protect yourself and your loved ones from falling victim to these deceitful schemes. Remember, staying informed and employing caution are your strongest defenses against lottery and prize scams in the modern digital landscape.

Chapter 14. Investment Scams and Pyramid Schemes

Introduction

In an era dominated by technological advancements and digital innovation, the realm of finance has experienced a significant transformation. While these changes have brought about numerous benefits, they have also opened the door to new avenues for fraudsters and scammers to exploit unsuspecting individuals. One of the most pervasive forms of financial deception is investment scams and pyramid schemes. In this article, we will delve into the intricacies of these fraudulent practices, explore their modus operandi, and provide insights into safeguarding oneself against falling victim to these schemes.

Understanding Investment Scams

Investment scams, also known as financial frauds or Ponzi schemes, represent a distressing threat to individuals seeking to grow their wealth through legitimate investments. These scams often come disguised as enticing opportunities promising high returns with minimal risk. The allure of quick and substantial profits can blind individuals to the underlying risks, making them vulnerable targets for scammers.

1. The Mechanics of Investment Scams

Investment scams typically involve a fraudulent individual or organization soliciting funds from investors, promising remarkable returns. The initial investors may indeed receive the promised returns, but these payouts are often sourced from the funds contributed by subsequent investors, rather than from any legitimate investment activities. The scheme collapses when there are insufficient new investments to cover the promised returns, leaving the majority of investors with significant losses.

2. Red Flags of Investment Scams

Guaranteed High Returns: Promises of guaranteed or unrealistically high returns are a hallmark of investment scams. Legitimate investments carry risk, and any offer that sounds too good to be true likely is.

Pressure to Invest Quickly: Scammers often create a sense of urgency, pressuring individuals to invest immediately before the supposed opportunity vanishes. Genuine investments should allow investors time to conduct thorough research.

Lack of Transparency: Scammers avoid providing detailed information about the investment strategy, risks, and how funds are used. Legitimate investments should offer clear and transparent information.

Decoding Pyramid Schemes

Pyramid schemes are a devious form of fraud that preys on individuals' desire to earn substantial income through recruitment and investment. These schemes have been adapted to the digital age, leveraging the power of social media and online platforms to widen their reach.

1. The Pyramid Structure

Pyramid schemes are built on a hierarchical structure where individuals at the top recruit new members who are required to invest a certain amount. These new members, in turn, recruit others, forming levels of participants. Participants are promised commissions for recruiting new members, creating an incentive to expand the pyramid. The scheme collapses when recruitment slows down, leaving those at the bottom with losses.

2. Identifying Pyramid Schemes

Emphasis on Recruitment: Pyramid schemes prioritize recruitment over the actual sale of products or services. If the focus is on recruiting new participants rather than selling a legitimate product, it's likely a pyramid scheme.

Entry Fees or Investments: Participants are often required to pay a fee to join or invest in the scheme. Legitimate business opportunities rarely require individuals to pay for the privilege of joining.

Unsustainable Income Promises: Pyramid schemes promise extravagant earnings with minimal effort. In reality, consistent and substantial income requires genuine work and effort.

Guarding Against Financial Deception

As the digital age continues to reshape the financial landscape, it's imperative to stay vigilant and informed to protect oneself from investment scams and pyramid schemes.

1. Conduct Thorough Research

Before investing in any opportunity, take the time to research the company, its founders, and the investment strategy. Legitimate businesses should have a clear track record and verifiable information.

2. Seek Professional Advice

Consulting with financial advisors or professionals before making investment decisions can provide valuable insights and help identify potential red flags.

3. Be Skeptical of Unrealistic Promises

Exercise caution when confronted with promises of guaranteed high returns or opportunities that seem too good to be true. Remember that all investments carry some level of risk.

4. Verify Credentials

Verify the credentials of individuals or organizations promoting investment opportunities. Legitimate investment professionals should have proper licenses and registrations.

5. Don't Succumb to Pressure

Resist the urge to make hasty decisions under pressure. Scammers often create a sense of urgency to prevent individuals from conducting due diligence.

6. Educate Yourself and Others

Spread awareness about investment scams and pyramid schemes to friends and family. Education is a powerful tool in preventing others from falling victim to fraud.

Conclusion

Investment scams and pyramid schemes continue to evolve, exploiting advancements in technology and communication. Staying informed, skeptical, and vigilant is crucial in safeguarding oneself against these deceptive practices. By understanding the mechanics of these schemes and recognizing the red flags, individuals can navigate the complex landscape of investments with greater confidence and resilience. In the digital age, arming oneself with knowledge is the most potent defense against financial deception.

Introduction

In the age of digital connectivity and instant communication, the noble act of charitable giving has been tainted by the emergence of charity scams. These scams exploit the goodwill of individuals and organizations by posing as legitimate charitable entities, with the sole intention of enriching fraudsters. As technology evolves, so do the tactics used by these scammers. This article explores the menace of charity scams in the digital age, shedding light on their methods, impact, and providing essential guidelines to safeguard against falling victim to such deceitful practices.

Understanding Charity Scams

1. Defining Charity Scams

Charity scams are deceptive practices wherein fraudsters masquerade as legitimate charitable organizations, soliciting donations or funds under false pretenses. These scams can take various forms, including online campaigns, cold calls, and even in-person interactions.

2. Motives Behind Charity Scams

Understanding the motives behind charity scams is crucial to comprehending their impact. Fraudsters engage in these scams to exploit people's generosity and sympathy, using emotional appeals to persuade individuals into making donations. The ill-gotten funds are often diverted for personal gain, leaving the intended beneficiaries deprived.

Common Tactics Employed by Charity Scammers

1. Emotional Manipulation

Charity scammers leverage heart-wrenching stories, compelling images, and emotionally charged language to evoke sympathy and compassion. This emotional manipulation is designed to override rational thinking, making individuals more susceptible to making impulsive donations.

2. Fake Websites and Online Campaigns

In the digital age, scammers create convincing websites and social media campaigns that closely mimic the branding and messaging of legitimate charities. They capitalize on the ease of online transactions, luring unsuspecting donors into contributing to fraudulent causes.

3. Phishing Emails and Cold Calls

Scammers send out phishing emails or make cold calls, claiming to represent well-known charitable organizations. These communications often contain urgent requests for donations or promises of helping a specific cause, leading recipients to provide their personal and financial information.

Impact of Charity Scams

1. Financial Losses

Victims of charity scams not only experience the loss of their hard-earned money but also the disappointment of realizing their contributions were diverted to criminal pockets instead of helping those in need.

2. Erosion of Trust

Charity scams erode public trust in genuine charitable organizations, making people skeptical about donating to legitimate causes. This erosion of trust has far-reaching implications for the philanthropic sector as a whole.

3. Harm to Legitimate Charities

The proliferation of charity scams can harm the reputation and effectiveness of legitimate charities, as donors become cautious or refrain from donating altogether due to fear of falling victim to scams.

Safeguarding Against Charity Scams

1. Research and Verification

Before making any donation, conduct thorough research to verify the authenticity of the charity. Check official websites, scrutinize financial records, and use reputable charity watchdog organizations to assess the legitimacy of the cause.

2. Direct Contact

Initiate contact with the charity directly through their official channels. Avoid responding to unsolicited emails, calls, or messages, as scammers often employ these methods to target potential victims.

3. Secure Online Transactions

When donating online, ensure the website is secure by checking for "https://" in the URL and looking for security certificates. Use trusted payment platforms and avoid sharing sensitive information over unsecured networks.

4. Be Wary of High-Pressure Tactics

Legitimate charities do not use high-pressure tactics to solicit donations. Be cautious if you feel rushed or manipulated into making a donation quickly.

5. Check for Tax-Exempt Status

Confirm the charity's tax-exempt status with relevant government agencies or watchdog organizations. Legitimate charities are registered and have proper documentation to prove their status.

Reporting and Taking Action

1. Reporting Suspected Scams

If you suspect a charity scam or have fallen victim to one, report it to the appropriate authorities, such as your local law enforcement agency, the Federal Trade Commission (FTC), or the Better Business Bureau (BBB).

2. Spreading Awareness

Help protect others by sharing information about charity scams with your friends, family, and social networks. By raising awareness, you contribute to preventing more individuals from becoming victims.

Conclusion

Charity scams remain a disheartening consequence of the digital age, exploiting the kindness and generosity of individuals for personal gain. However, armed with knowledge and vigilance, we can collectively safeguard against falling victim to these fraudulent practices. By understanding the tactics employed by scammers, recognizing the signs of a potential charity scam, and taking proactive measures to verify the legitimacy of charitable organizations, we can ensure that our well-intentioned donations truly make a positive impact in the lives of those in need. It is incumbent upon us to protect the spirit of philanthropy and uphold the values of compassion and altruism, even in the face of the ever-evolving landscape of digital fraud.

Introduction

In an era where technological advancements have transformed the way we live, work, and communicate, the digital landscape offers unprecedented opportunities for convenience and connectivity. However, this digital revolution has also given rise to an alarming surge in cybercrime, with scams and frauds becoming increasingly sophisticated and insidious. Among these, one of the most menacing threats that has gained traction in recent times is AI-enhanced credential stuffing, a cyberattack technique that poses a grave danger to individuals and organizations alike.

The Digital Age's Dark Side

As our lives intertwine further with the digital realm, the risks of cyber threats have grown exponentially. The convenience of online banking, shopping, and social networking has created a treasure trove of valuable data, making individuals and businesses vulnerable to various forms of cybercrime. While traditional methods of hacking and phishing remain prevalent, the emergence of AI-enhanced credential stuffing takes cybercriminal activity to a new level of sophistication.

Understanding Credential Stuffing

Credential stuffing, at its core, is a brute-force attack method where cybercriminals exploit the practice of using the same username and password combinations across multiple online platforms. Armed with a database of stolen or leaked credentials, hackers use automated tools to systematically bombard websites with these login combinations until they gain unauthorized access. This technique thrives on individuals' tendency to reuse passwords, leading to the compromise of numerous accounts across different platforms.

The Evolution of AI in Cyberattacks

The integration of artificial intelligence (AI) in cyberattacks marks a significant advancement in the realm of digital fraud. AI empowers cybercriminals to fine-tune their attack strategies by leveraging sophisticated algorithms that can quickly adapt to evolving security measures. AI's ability to analyze vast amounts of data enables hackers to refine their target selection, timing, and execution, rendering traditional defense mechanisms obsolete.

The Convergence

AI-enhanced credential stuffing leverages the capabilities of AI to automate and optimize the credential stuffing process. By incorporating machine learning algorithms, hackers can better predict patterns, detect anomalies, and customize attack vectors based on the victim's behavior and online activities. This fusion of AI and credential stuffing amplifies the scale and potency of cyberattacks, resulting in a higher success rate for hackers and greater devastation for victims.

Unveiling the Mechanism

1. Data Harvesting and Enrichment: Hackers gather vast datasets of stolen credentials from previous breaches or the

dark web. AI is employed to analyze and categorize this data, identifying patterns and trends that aid in selecting potential targets.

2. Behavioral Analysis: AI algorithms scrutinize users' online behaviors, including browsing habits, social media activity, and purchase history. This information is used to create a detailed profile, allowing attackers to tailor their tactics and make the attack seem more legitimate.

3. Automated Attacks: With the refined datasets and personalized profiles, hackers use AI-driven tools to automate login attempts across multiple websites. The AI continuously adapts its approach based on the results, making it increasingly difficult for traditional security measures to detect or prevent the attack.

4. Credential Validation: As the attack progresses, the AI identifies successful logins and validates compromised credentials. These validated credentials are then utilized for further unauthorized access or sold on the dark web, perpetuating a vicious cycle of cybercrime.

The Impending Threat

The repercussions of AI-enhanced credential stuffing are far-reaching and can have dire consequences for individuals and businesses alike:

1. Financial Loss: Unauthorized access to bank accounts, credit cards, and digital wallets can lead to significant financial losses for individuals. Businesses may also face financial repercussions due to fraudulent transactions and legal liabilities.

2. Identity Theft: Compromised accounts provide cybercriminals with a treasure trove of personal information, enabling identity theft and the potential for more elaborate scams.

3. Reputation Damage: Individuals and organizations can suffer irreparable damage to their reputation as a result of cyberattacks, leading to loss of trust and credibility.

4. Data Breaches: Successful AI-enhanced credential stuffing attacks can pave the way for data breaches, exposing sensitive information and undermining data privacy.

5. Operational Disruption: For businesses, credential stuffing attacks can disrupt operations, strain customer relations, and incur significant recovery costs.

Mitigating the Threat

1. Password Hygiene: Encouraging users to practice good password hygiene, such as using strong and unique passwords for each account, can significantly reduce the success rate of credential stuffing attacks.

2. Multi-Factor Authentication (MFA): Implementing MFA adds an extra layer of security by requiring users to provide multiple forms of verification, making it harder for cybercriminals to gain unauthorized access.

3. User and Entity Behavior Analytics (UEBA): UEBA is a security approach that utilizes advanced analytics to monitor and detect anomalous behaviors of users and entities within an organization's network to identify potential security threats or risks. UEBA solutions employ

AI to monitor user behaviors and detect anomalies, helping to identify potential credential stuffing attacks in real-time.

4. Rate Limiting and CAPTCHAs: Rate limiting is a mechanism that restricts the number of requests or actions a user or IP address can perform within a specified time frame to prevent abuse or overload. CAPTCHA (Completely Automated Public Turing test to tell Computers and Humans Apart) is a challenge designed to differentiate between human users and automated bots, often involving tasks that are easy for humans but difficult for bots to solve. Implementing rate limiting and CAPTCHA challenges can thwart automated attacks by slowing down the login process and verifying human users.

5. Regular Security Audits: Individuals and businesses should conduct routine security audits to identify vulnerabilities and implement timely security patches and updates.

Conclusion

As the digital age continues to evolve, so do the methods and techniques employed by cybercriminals. AI-enhanced credential stuffing represents a formidable threat that demands immediate attention and concerted efforts from individuals, businesses, and cybersecurity experts. By staying informed, adopting robust security measures, and embracing technological innovations, we can collectively safeguard against the rising tide of scams and frauds in the digital age. The battle against AI-enhanced credential stuffing is a critical one, and only through collaborative vigilance can we ensure a safer digital future for all.

Introduction

In today's digitally driven world, where information and communication flow seamlessly across various platforms, the threat of scams and frauds has reached unprecedented levels. One of the most insidious forms of deception that has emerged in the digital age is impersonation scams. Impersonation scams involve the cunning manipulation of trust and identity, exploiting individuals' vulnerabilities and naivety for financial gain. This article delves deep into the realm of impersonation scams, shedding light on their various forms, tactics employed by scammers, and most importantly, how individuals can safeguard themselves against these deceitful ploys.

Understanding Impersonation Scams

Impersonation scams encompass a range of fraudulent activities where perpetrators assume false identities to deceive victims into parting with their money, sensitive information, or even their dignity. These scams are orchestrated through various channels, including emails, social media, phone calls, and even in-person interactions. By leveraging familiarity, authority, or emotional manipulation, scammers create an illusion of legitimacy, making it difficult for victims to discern the fraudulent nature of the interaction.

Common Forms of Impersonation Scams

As detailed in earlier chapters of this book, the following are common forms of impersonation scams:

1. Phishing Scams: A pervasive form of impersonation scam, phishing involves sending fraudulent emails, messages, or websites that imitate trusted entities, like banks, government agencies, or reputable companies. These messages often request personal or financial information under the guise of urgent account updates or security measures.

2. Tech Support Scams: Scammers impersonate technical support personnel from well-known technology companies and contact victims to offer assistance in fixing non-existent computer issues. They often coerce victims into granting remote access to their devices or paying for unnecessary software and services.

3. Romance Scams: Playing on emotional vulnerabilities, scammers create fake online personas, often in the form of potential romantic partners. They establish deep connections with victims, only to later request money for various fabricated reasons, exploiting the victim's feelings and trust.

4. CEO/Business Email Compromise (BEC) Scams: Scammers target businesses by impersonating company executives or high-ranking officials. They manipulate employees into transferring funds or divulging confidential information, under the pretext of urgent business matters.

5. Social Media Impersonation: Fraudsters create fake profiles on social media platforms, imitating celebrities, influencers, or even friends and family. These imposters then solicit money, personal information, or engage in other deceitful activities under the guise of the impersonated individual.

6. Government Impersonation Scams: Scammers impersonate government officials, law enforcement officers, or tax agencies, claiming that the victim owes money or is involved in illegal activities. They threaten legal consequences unless immediate payment is made.

Tactics Employed by Impersonation Scammers

1. Emotional Manipulation: Scammers exploit human emotions, such as fear, compassion, and urgency, to cloud judgment and elicit desired responses from victims. Whether through creating a sense of impending danger or tugging at heartstrings, emotional manipulation is a powerful tool in their arsenal.

2. Authority and Trust: Impersonators often present themselves as figures of authority, leveraging titles, uniforms, or official language to gain victims' trust. By appearing to be legitimate individuals, scammers succeed in breaking down skepticism.

3. Urgency and Time Pressure: Many impersonation scams rely on creating a sense of urgency, leaving victims with little time to think critically. Urgent requests for financial transactions or information often push victims into making hasty decisions.

4. Spoofing and Camouflage: Scammers employ advanced tactics like caller ID spoofing, email domain impersonation, and fake websites to mimic the appearance of trusted entities. These techniques further deceive victims into believing they are interacting with genuine sources.

Safeguarding Against Impersonation Scams

1. Education and Awareness: Knowledge is the first line of defense. Individuals should familiarize themselves with common impersonation scam tactics and be cautious when approached with urgent or unexpected requests for personal or financial information.

2. Verification Protocols: Before acting on any requests, individuals should independently verify the identity of the person or entity contacting them. This can be done by using official contact details from trusted sources, rather than relying on information provided in unsolicited communications.

3. Secure Communication Channels: Whenever possible, communicate through secure platforms and channels. Ensure that websites have "https" in their URLs and double-check email addresses and sender information.

4. Two-Factor Authentication (2FA): Enable 2FA on important accounts to add an extra layer of security. Even if scammers have access to login credentials, they would still need a second form of verification to gain access.

5. Guard Personal Information: Be cautious about sharing personal or financial information, especially over the phone or via email. Legitimate entities rarely ask for sensitive information through these channels.

6. Independent Confirmation: If approached by someone claiming to be a friend or family member in need, independently confirm their situation through another trusted means of communication before taking any action.

7. Report Suspicious Activity: If something feels off or too good to be true, report it to the appropriate authorities. Reporting scams can help prevent others from falling victim to similar tactics.

Conclusion

Impersonation scams are a pervasive and evolving threat that preys on human psychology and trust. As digital interactions become more ingrained in our daily lives, the risk of falling victim to these scams increases. By understanding the various forms of impersonation scams, recognizing their tactics, and adopting proactive measures, individuals can empower themselves to navigate the digital landscape safely. Vigilance, education, and a healthy dose of skepticism are essential tools in the fight against impersonation scams, ensuring a more secure and resilient digital age for all.

Introduction

In the ever-evolving landscape of the digital age, technological advancements have brought forth a plethora of benefits and conveniences. However, this progress has also given rise to new avenues for scams and frauds. Among these, AI chatbot money doublers have emerged as a particularly insidious threat, exploiting the trust and curiosity of unsuspecting individuals. This article delves into the realm of AI chatbot money doublers, dissecting their tactics, impacts, and the imperative need for safeguarding against them.

The Allure of Quick Wealth

1. The Promise of Instant Doubling

The core allure of AI chatbot money doublers lies in their enticing promise of multiplying one's wealth within an unbelievably short period. This appeal to human greed and the desire for quick riches has proven to be a powerful psychological trigger.

2. Psychological Manipulation

These scams employ advanced AI algorithms to simulate human-like conversations, leveraging persuasive language and emotional manipulation to convince users that they can double or even triple their investments effortlessly.

The Mechanics Behind AI Chatbot Money Doublers

1. Technological Facade

AI chatbot money doublers rely on advanced natural language processing (NLP) and machine learning algorithms to create a facade of legitimacy. These bots can engage in seemingly intelligent conversations, fostering a false sense of trust.

2. Algorithmic Deception

The algorithms used by these scams are designed to exploit cognitive biases, such as confirmation bias and scarcity mentality. By tailoring responses to individual users, the chatbots create a sense of personalization, further enhancing their deceptive tactics.

Unveiling the Red Flags

1. Overemphasis on Urgency

One common red flag is the exaggerated emphasis on time sensitivity. Scammers often deploy urgency tactics, pressuring users to invest quickly before a purported "golden opportunity" vanishes.

2. Lack of Transparency

AI chatbot money doublers deliberately obfuscate the details of their operations, making it difficult for users to understand how their money is being invested or doubled. Lack of transparency is a telltale sign of a potential scam.

3. Unrealistic Returns

Promising unrealistic and consistent returns on investments is a hallmark of these scams. Any investment opportunity that sounds too good to be true should be approached with skepticism.

The Human Element: Exploiting Vulnerabilities

1. Exploiting Emotional Vulnerabilities

Scammers leverage emotions like fear of missing out (FOMO) and the hope for financial freedom to manipulate users into parting with their money. They create a sense of urgency and belonging to lure victims into their schemes.

2. Social Proof and Bandwagon Effect

AI chatbot money doublers often present fabricated testimonials and user success stories to create a false sense of legitimacy. The bandwagon effect refers to the tendency for people to adopt certain behaviors or beliefs because they perceive them to be popular or widely accepted. Users may be swayed by the bandwagon effect, assuming that if others have succeeded, they will too.

Real-world Impacts

1. Financial Losses

The most immediate impact of falling victim to an AI chatbot money doubler is the financial loss incurred by the unsuspecting individuals who invest their hard-earned money in these scams.

Beyond financial losses, victims often suffer from psychological distress, including feelings of shame, guilt, and anger. These emotional consequences can have a lasting impact on an individual's well-being.

Safeguarding Against AI Chatbot Money Doublers

1. Education and Awareness

Raising awareness about the existence and tactics of AI chatbot money doublers is crucial. Educating individuals about red flags, common strategies, and the importance of due diligence can empower them to make informed decisions.

2. Skepticism and Due Diligence

Encouraging a healthy dose of skepticism is essential. Individuals should conduct thorough research, verify claims, and seek advice from financial experts before making any investment decisions.

3. Technological Countermeasures

The tech industry and cybersecurity experts play a vital role in developing tools to identify and counteract AI chatbot money doublers. Advanced algorithms and AI-driven solutions can help detect and block such scams before they reach potential victims.

Conclusion

AI chatbot money doublers exemplify the dark side of technological progress, capitalizing on human vulnerabilities for financial gain. As the digital landscape continues to evolve, safeguarding against scams and frauds becomes increasingly important. By understanding the mechanics of these scams, recognizing red flags, and promoting education and awareness, individuals can navigate the digital age with greater resilience and protect themselves from falling prey to the deceptive clutches of AI chatbot money doublers.

Introduction

In today's interconnected digital age, where technology continues to reshape our lives, the rise of online scams and frauds has become an alarming concern. One particularly sinister and distressing form of digital exploitation is the "Porn Video Call Scam" – a malicious scheme designed to manipulate individuals into compromising situations and extorting money or personal information through blackmail. This article delves into the insidious world of porn video call scams and blackmailing, aiming to educate readers about the tactics used by scammers and empower them with knowledge to safeguard themselves against these threats.

Understanding Porn Video Call Scams

1. The Anatomy of a Scam

Porn video call scams typically begin with a seemingly harmless online interaction, often on social media platforms, dating apps, or chat rooms. Scammers befriend their victims and establish a level of trust, exploiting vulnerabilities, and eliciting personal information.

2. The Entrapment

Scammers then escalate the interaction, convincing the victim to engage in explicit or sexual conversations and activities on video calls. Unbeknownst to the victim, these interactions are recorded for later use in blackmail.

3. The Blackmail Phase

Once the scammer has compromising video content, they reveal their true intent – to blackmail the victim. The victim is threatened with exposure of the explicit material to their friends, family, or colleagues unless a ransom is paid.

Common Tactics Employed by Scammers

1. Social Engineering

Scammers use psychological manipulation to exploit emotions, such as loneliness, curiosity, or desire for companionship, to establish a connection and gain the victim's trust.

2. Impersonation and Catfishing

Scammers often create fake profiles, assuming false identities to build rapport. They may impersonate potential romantic partners or acquaintances to lower the victim's guard.

3. Grooming and Emotional Investment

Over time, scammers invest effort in building an emotional connection with the victim, making them feel valued and understood. This emotional investment makes the victim more susceptible to manipulation.

4. Coercion and Threats

Once explicit content is obtained, scammers resort to threats of public exposure, shame, and humiliation to force victims into compliance.

5. Fake Video Technology

Scammers may use deepfake technology or pre-recorded videos to simulate live interactions, making it difficult for victims to distinguish between genuine and manipulated content.

Impact and Consequences

1. Psychological Distress

Victims of porn video call scams often suffer from severe emotional trauma, anxiety, and depression due to the fear of public humiliation and exposure.

2. Financial Loss

Many victims succumb to the blackmail demands, leading to significant financial losses as scammers continue to exploit their vulnerability.

3. Personal and Professional Repercussions

The exposure of explicit content can have devastating consequences on personal relationships, careers, and reputation.

Safeguarding Against Porn Video Call Scams

1. Digital Literacy and Awareness

Education is the first line of defense. Stay informed about various online scams and frauds, and be skeptical of online interactions that seem too good to be true.

2. Privacy Settings and Secure Platforms

Review and adjust privacy settings on social media platforms and dating apps to limit the amount of personal information shared. Use reputable and secure platforms for online interactions.

3. Identity Verification

Whenever possible, verify the identity of individuals you interact with online before sharing personal information or engaging in video calls.

4. Avoid Explicit Content Sharing

Refrain from sharing explicit content during online interactions, as scammers can use such material against you.

5. Two-Factor Authentication (2FA)

Enable 2FA on your accounts to add an extra layer of security and prevent unauthorized access.

6. Regularly Update Passwords

Change passwords regularly and use strong, unique passwords for different accounts to minimize the risk of hacking.

7. Be Cautious of Requests

Be wary of requests for money, personal information, or explicit content, especially from individuals you've only interacted with online.

Report any suspicious or threatening behavior to the relevant platform or authorities to help prevent further victimization.

Conclusion

Porn video call scams and blackmailing are distressing forms of digital exploitation that can have far-reaching consequences on individuals' lives. By understanding the tactics employed by scammers, raising awareness, and adopting proactive security measures, we can collectively work towards safeguarding ourselves and our digital communities against these insidious threats. In an era where technology facilitates both connections and vulnerabilities, arming ourselves with knowledge and vigilance is crucial to navigate the digital landscape safely and with confidence.

Chapter 20. Protecting Yourself from Scams and Fraud

Introduction

In an increasingly digitized world, the convenience and connectivity offered by technology have opened up new avenues for communication, commerce, and interaction. However, along with these benefits come the lurking threats of scams and frauds that can jeopardize your financial well-being, personal information, and even your sense of security. The rapid evolution of digital tools and techniques has made it easier for scammers and fraudsters to target unsuspecting individuals. In this article, we will delve into the strategies and precautions you can take to protect yourself from scams and frauds in the digital age.

The Rising Threat of Scams and Frauds

The digital age has ushered in unparalleled convenience and efficiency, but it has also given rise to a plethora of scams and frauds that exploit technological vulnerabilities and human psychology. Scammers have become adept at using various techniques to manipulate individuals into divulging personal information, making unauthorized financial transactions, or falling victim to identity theft. These scams can range from sophisticated phishing emails to fraudulent investment schemes. It is crucial to understand these threats and arm yourself with knowledge to safeguard against them.

Recognizing Common Scams and Frauds

Awareness is the first line of defense against scams and frauds. Familiarizing yourself with common tactics scammers employ can help you identify potential threats. Some prevalent scams include:

1. Phishing: Scammers impersonate legitimate entities to trick you into revealing sensitive information, such as passwords or credit card details, often through deceptive emails or websites.

2. Impersonation Scams: Fraudsters pose as government officials, company representatives, or even family members to manipulate you into sending money or sharing personal data.

3. Investment Scams: Scammers promise high returns on investments that seem too good to be true, often luring victims through persuasive sales pitches.

4. Tech Support Scams: Scammers claim to be tech support personnel from reputable companies and manipulate you into granting them remote access to your computer, enabling them to steal sensitive information.

5. Romance Scams: Scammers develop fake online relationships to emotionally manipulate victims into sending money or providing financial assistance.

Strengthening Digital Literacy

Developing strong digital literacy is paramount in today's landscape. Understanding how digital platforms work and being able to discern genuine from fake information can significantly reduce your vulnerability to scams and frauds. Here's how you can enhance your digital literacy:

1. Verify Information: Always cross-check information from multiple sources before taking any action, especially if it involves sharing personal or financial details.

2. Educate Yourself: Stay informed about new scams and fraud trends. Government agencies and consumer protection organizations often publish alerts and resources to help you recognize and avoid scams.

3. Secure Browsing: Ensure that websites you visit are secure (look for "https" in the URL and a padlock symbol), and avoid clicking on suspicious links.

4. Email Vigilance: Be cautious when clicking on links or downloading attachments from unknown senders. Hover over links to see their destination before clicking.

Fortifying Your Personal Information

Your personal information is a valuable target for scammers. Safeguarding it should be a top priority:

1. Strong Passwords: Use unique and strong passwords for all your online accounts. Consider using a password manager to keep track of them securely.

2. Two-Factor Authentication (2FA): Enable 2FA whenever possible. This adds an extra layer of security by requiring a second form of verification, such as a text message or authentication app, in addition to your password.

3. Privacy Settings: Adjust privacy settings on social media platforms and other online accounts to limit the amount of personal information visible to the public.

4. Be Cautious with Personal Details: Be wary of sharing personal information on social media or other public forums, as scammers can use these details to create convincing impersonations.

Navigating Financial Transactions

Financial transactions in the digital age offer convenience, but they also open avenues for fraud. Here's how you can protect your financial well-being:

1. Secure Networks: Avoid conducting financial transactions on public Wi-Fi networks. Use secure, password-protected networks when handling sensitive information.

2. Regular Account Monitoring: Frequently review your bank and credit card statements for unauthorized transactions. Report any discrepancies promptly.

3. Beware of Requests for Money: Be skeptical of unsolicited requests for money, even if they appear to be from friends or family. Verify such requests through a separate communication channel.

4. Secure Online Shopping: Only purchase from reputable websites with secure payment gateways. Look for the padlock symbol and "https" in the URL.

Staying Skeptical and Seeking Help

A healthy dose of skepticism can go a long way in protecting yourself from scams and frauds:

1. Trust Your Instincts: If something feels too good to be true or raises suspicions, it probably is. Trust your gut feelings and approach offers with caution.

2. Seek Professional Advice: If you're unsure about an investment opportunity or financial transaction, consult a trusted financial advisor or legal expert before proceeding.

3. Report Suspicious Activity: If you encounter a scam or believe you've been targeted, report it to the appropriate authorities, such as the Federal Trade Commission (FTC) or your local law enforcement agency.

Conclusion

The digital age has redefined the way we interact, work, and conduct transactions. While it brings immense opportunities, it also exposes us to the growing threat of scams and frauds. By arming ourselves with knowledge, cultivating strong digital literacy, and adopting cautious behaviors, we can significantly reduce the risk of falling victim to these malicious schemes. Protecting yourself from scams and frauds is not just about safeguarding your finances; it's about preserving your peace of mind and maintaining control over your digital life. As technology continues to advance, our vigilance and proactive measures become even more crucial in ensuring a safe and secure digital future.

Introduction

In an increasingly digitized world, where technology evolves at a rapid pace, the landscape of scams and frauds is also evolving. As society embraces new technologies, so do criminals find innovative ways to exploit them. The battle against scams and frauds is a never-ending one, requiring constant vigilance, adaptation, and innovation. In this article, we delve into the future trends in scams and fraud prevention, exploring how emerging technologies and changing tactics will shape the landscape of digital security.

The Digital Age and the Rising Threat of Scams and Frauds

The digital age has brought about remarkable advancements, transforming the way we live, work, and interact. However, this era of convenience and connectivity has also given rise to an alarming increase in scams and frauds. Cybercriminals exploit vulnerabilities in technology, psychology, and human behavior to target unsuspecting individuals and organizations. As we look ahead, it's imperative to identify and understand the future trends that will define the realm of scams and frauds prevention.

Artificial Intelligence and Machine Learning in Fraud Detection

Artificial Intelligence (AI) and Machine Learning (ML) have already made significant strides in various industries, and their potential in fraud prevention is immense. These technologies can analyze vast amounts of data, identify patterns, and detect anomalies that might indicate fraudulent activities. AI-powered systems can learn from new data and adapt to evolving scam tactics, making them a formidable weapon against cybercriminals.

Furthermore, AI can be used to enhance user authentication processes. Facial recognition, voice biometrics, and behavioral analytics can create multi-layered security barriers, making it much harder for fraudsters to breach systems. As AI continues to advance, its role in preventing scams and frauds is likely to become even more pivotal.

Biometric Authentication and Identification

Biometric authentication methods, such as fingerprints, iris scans, and facial recognition, offer a promising avenue for fraud prevention. These unique physical and behavioral traits provide a higher level of security than traditional passwords or PINs. As the technology becomes more refined and widely adopted, it could significantly reduce instances of identity theft and unauthorized access.

Additionally, biometric data can be used to verify the authenticity of transactions. For instance, a user's fingerprint could be used to confirm a financial transfer, adding an extra layer of security against unauthorized transactions. As biometric technology matures, it may revolutionize the way we interact with digital systems, making scams and frauds more challenging to execute.

Quantum Computing and Encryption

Quantum computing harnesses the principles of quantum mechanics to perform complex calculations that traditional computers struggle with. While quantum computing holds immense potential for solving complex problems, it also poses a threat to traditional encryption methods. Quantum computers can theoretically break current encryption codes, jeopardizing the security of sensitive data and transactions. However, this challenge also presents an opportunity for innovation.

Researchers are actively working on quantum-resistant encryption techniques that can withstand the power of quantum computers. These new encryption methods will play a crucial role in safeguarding digital systems against future threats. As quantum computing becomes more prevalent, investing in quantum-resistant encryption will be vital for staying ahead of cybercriminals.

Enhanced Data Privacy and Regulation

Data breaches and privacy violations have become all too common in today's digital landscape. In response, governments around the world are implementing stricter data protection regulations, such as the European Union's General Data Protection Regulation (GDPR) and the California Consumer Privacy Act (CCPA). These regulations empower individuals with greater control over their personal data and hold organizations accountable for its protection.

In the future, we can expect more comprehensive and stringent data privacy laws to emerge. Organizations will need to adopt advanced cybersecurity measures, implement transparent data practices, and prioritize user consent. The convergence of technology and regulation will create a safer online environment, reducing the avenues through which scammers and fraudsters operate.

Behavioral Analytics and Predictive Modeling

Understanding human behavior is a key aspect of fraud prevention. Behavioral analytics and predictive modeling leverage data to identify unusual or suspicious activities based on user behavior patterns. By monitoring interactions, transactions, and navigation patterns, these techniques can detect deviations from normal behavior that might indicate a scam or fraud attempt.

As AI and ML algorithms improve, behavioral analytics will become more accurate and sophisticated. Systems will be able to identify subtle changes in behavior that are indicative of fraudulent activities. This proactive approach to fraud prevention will play a significant role in mitigating risks in the digital age.

Social Engineering and Psychological Manipulation

While technological advancements are crucial in fraud prevention, social engineering and psychological manipulation remain potent tools in a scammer's arsenal. Cybercriminals exploit human emotions, biases, and cognitive vulnerabilities to deceive individuals into revealing sensitive information or performing actions that benefit the scammer.

To combat this, education and awareness will be vital. Individuals and organizations must be educated about the tactics used by scammers and trained to recognize red flags. By fostering a culture of skepticism and critical thinking, we can reduce the effectiveness of social engineering attacks.

Blockchain Technology for Transparent Transactions

Blockchain technology is a decentralized and secure digital ledger system for recording and verifying transactions. Blockchain, originally known for powering cryptocurrencies, has far-reaching applications beyond the financial sector. Its decentralized and transparent nature can revolutionize various industries, including supply chain management, healthcare, and digital identity verification.

In the realm of fraud prevention, blockchain's immutability can ensure the integrity of transactions and records. It can create an unalterable ledger of activities, making it nearly impossible for fraudsters to manipulate data. As blockchain technology evolves and gains wider acceptance, it will introduce new layers of security to digital interactions.

Conclusion

As the digital age continues to evolve, the fight against scams and frauds will require a multi-faceted approach. The convergence of AI, biometrics, quantum-resistant encryption, data privacy regulations, behavioral analytics, and blockchain technology will shape the future of fraud prevention. While technology will play a pivotal role, human vigilance, education, and awareness remain equally crucial.

The landscape of scams and frauds is ever-changing, with cybercriminals continuously adapting their tactics to exploit vulnerabilities. By staying informed, embracing emerging technologies, and fostering a culture of cybersecurity, we can safeguard against scams and frauds in the digital age and ensure a safer online environment for all. The future of fraud prevention is dynamic, challenging, and full of opportunities to innovate and stay one step ahead of those who seek to exploit our vulnerabilities.

In this comprehensive guide, "Safeguarding Against Scams and Frauds in the Digital Age," readers will delve into the ever-evolving world of cybercrime and learn how to protect themselves from the multitude of scams and frauds that plague the digital landscape. The book starts with Chapter 1, providing a compelling introduction to the prevalent threat of scams and frauds in the modern era. Subsequent chapters explore specific areas of concern, including identity theft, phishing scams, and the emerging dangers of smishing and vishing. The author then delves into the realm of fake social media profiles and catfishing, followed by an in-depth analysis of romance scams and the disturbing rise of AI-generated fake content, known as deepfakes. The impact of AI is further examined in chapters on chatbot scams, AI-driven robocalls, and AI-powered phishing and social engineering.

As readers progress through the book, they gain insights into AI-enhanced scams like business email compromise and online auction fraud, along with the persistent threats of lottery and prize scams, investment scams, and pyramid schemes. Furthermore, the author addresses the concerning reality of charity scams, AI-enhanced credential stuffing, impersonation scams, and AI chatbot money doublers. Shedding light on the alarming trend of porn video call scams and blackmailing, the book concludes with Chapter 20, offering practical guidance on how individuals can protect themselves from these digital menaces. The book's final chapter, Chapter 21, looks to the future, examining the evolving landscape of scams and fraud prevention, and how technology and awareness can work in tandem to stay one step ahead of cybercriminals. With expert insights and actionable advice, "Safeguarding Against Scams and Frauds in the Digital Age" equips readers with the necessary tools to navigate the digital realm safely and confidently.

ABOUT THE AUTHOR

Mr. C. P. Kumar is a retired Scientist 'G' from National Institute of Hydrology, Roorkee, Uttarakhand, India. He is also a Reiki Healer and Chakra Balancing practitioner (with pendulum dowsing) and offers Emotional Freedom Technique (EFT) to help individuals with emotional issues. Mr. Kumar has authored many books on technical, spiritual, and social topics.

For further details, you may visit his webpage
https://www.angelfire.com/nh/cpkumar/virgo.html